J 953.3
Marco
Marcovitz, Hal

Yemen

Major Muslim Nations

YEMEN

Major Muslim Nations

YEMEN

HAL MARCOVITZ

MASON CREST PUBLISHERS
PHILADELPHIA

Mason Crest Publishers
370 Reed Road
Broomall, PA 19008
www.masoncrest.com

Copyright © 2010 by Mason Crest Publishers. All rights reserved.
Printed and bound in the Hashemite Kingdom of Jordan.

First printing

1 3 5 7 9 8 6 4 2

Library of Congress Cataloging-in-Publication Data

Marcovitz, Hal.
  Yemen / Hal Marcovitz.
      p. cm. — (Major Muslim Nations)
    ISBN 978-1-4222-1396-4 (hardcover) — ISBN 978-1-4222-1426-8 (pbk.)
    1. Yemen (Republic)—Juvenile literature. I. Title.
    DS247.Y48M253 2008
    953.3—dc22
                                              2008041227

Original ISBN: 1-59084-521-8 (hc)

Major Muslim Nations

TABLE OF CONTENTS

Major Muslim Nations

Dr. Harvey Sicherman, president and director of the Foreign Policy Research Institute, is the author of such books as *America the Vulnerable: Our Military Problems and How to Fix Them* (2002) and *Palestinian Autonomy, Self-Government and Peace* (1993).

Introduction

by Dr. Harvey Sicherman

America's triumph in the Cold War promised a new burst of peace and prosperity. Indeed, the decade between the demise of the Soviet Union and the destruction of September 11, 2001, seems in retrospect deceptively attractive. Today, of course, we are more fully aware—to our sorrow—of the dangers and troubles no longer just below the surface.

The Muslim identities of most of the terrorists at war with the United States have also provoked great interest in Islam and the role of religion in politics. A truly global religion, Islam's tenets are held by hundreds of millions of people from every ethnic group, scattered across the globe. It is crucial for Americans not to assume that Osama bin Laden's ideas are identical to those of most Muslims, or, for that matter, that most Muslims are Arabs. Also, it is important for Americans to understand the "hot spots" in the Muslim world because many will make an impact on the United States.

A glance at the map establishes the extraordinary coverage of our authors. Every climate and terrain may be found and every form of human society, from the nomads of the Central Asian steppes and Arabian deserts to highly sophisticated cities such as Cairo and Singapore. Economies range from barter systems to stock exchanges, from oil-rich countries to the thriving semi-market powers, such as India, now on the march. Others have built wealth on service and shipping.

The Middle East and Central Asia are heavily armed and turbulent. Pakistan is a nuclear power, Iran threatens to become one, and Israel is assumed to possess a small arsenal. But in other places, such as Afghanistan and the Sudan, the horse and mule remain potent instruments of war. All have a rich history of conflict, domestic and international, old and new.

Governments include dictatorships, democracies, and hybrids without a name; centralized and decentralized administrations; and older patterns of tribal and clan associations. The region is a veritable encyclopedia of political expression.

Although such variety defies easy generalities, it is still possible to make several observations.

First, the regional geopolitics reflect the impact of empires and the struggles of post-imperial independence. While centuries-old history is often invoked, the truth is that the modern Middle East political system dates only from the 1920s, when the Ottoman Empire dissolved in the wake of its defeat by Britain and France in World War I. States such as Algeria, Iraq, Israel, Jordan, Kuwait, Saudi Arabia, Syria, Turkey, and the United Arab Emirates did not exist before 1914—they became independent between 1920 and 1971. Others, such as Egypt and Iran, were dominated by foreign powers until well after World War II. Few of the leaders of these states were happy with the territories they were assigned or the borders, which were often drawn by Europeans. Yet the system has endured despite many efforts to change it.

A similar story may be told in South Asia. The British Raj dissolved into India and Pakistan in 1947. Still further east, Malaysia shares a British experience but Indonesia, a Dutch invention, has its own European heritage. These imperial histories weigh heavily upon the politics of the region.

The second observation concerns economics, demography, and natural resources. These countries offer dramatic geographical contrasts: vast parched deserts and high mountains, some with year-round snow; stone-hard volcanic rifts and lush semi-tropical valleys; extremely dry and extremely wet conditions, sometimes separated by only a few miles; large permanent rivers and wadis, riverbeds dry as a bone until winter rains send torrents of flood from the mountains to the sea.

Although famous historically for its exports of grains, fabrics, and spices, most recently the Muslim regions are known more for a single commodity: oil. Petroleum is unevenly distributed; while it is largely concentrated in the Persian Gulf and Arabian Peninsula, large oil fields can be found in Algeria, Libya, and further east in Indonesia. Natural gas is also abundant in the Gulf, and there are new, potentially lucrative offshore gas fields in the Eastern Mediterranean.

This uneven distribution of wealth has been compounded by demographics. Birth rates are very high, but the countries with the most oil are often lightly populated. Over the last decade, a youth "bulge" has emerged and this, combined with increased urbanization, has strained water supplies, air quality, public sanitation, and health services throughout the Muslim world. How will these young people be educated? Where will they work? A large outward migration, especially to Europe, indicates the lack of opportunity at home.

In the face of these challenges, the traditional state-dominated economic strategies have given way partly to experiments with "privatization" and foreign investment. But economic progress has come slowly, if at all, and most people have yet to benefit from "globalization," although there are pockets of prosperity, high technology (notably in Israel), and valuable natural resources (oil, gas, and minerals). Rising expectations have yet to be met.

A third important observation is the role of religion in the Middle East. Americans, who take separation of church and state for granted, should know that most countries in the region either proclaim their countries to be Muslim or allow a very large role for that religion in public life. (Islamic law, Sharia, permits people to practice Judaism and Christianity in Muslim states but only as *dhimmi*, "protected" but second-class citizens.) Among those with predominantly Muslim populations, Turkey alone describes itself as secular and prohibits avowedly religious parties in the political system. Lebanon was a Christian-dominated state, and Israel continues to be a Jewish state. Even where politics are secular, religion plays an enormous role in culture, daily life, and legislation.

Islam has deeply affected every state and people in these regions. But Islamic practices and groups vary from the well-known Sunni and Shiite groups to energetic Salafi (Wahhabi) and Sufi movements. Over the last 20 years especially, South and Central Asia have become battlegrounds for competing Shiite (Iranian) and Wahhabi (Saudi) doctrines, well financed from abroad and aggressively antagonistic toward non-Muslims and each other. Resistance to the Soviet war in Afghanistan brought these groups battle-tested warriors and organizers responsive to the doctrines made popular by Osama bin Laden and others. This newly significant struggle within Islam, superimposed on an older Muslim history, will shape political and economic destinies throughout the region and beyond.

We hope that these books will enlighten both teacher and student about the critical "hot spots" of the Muslim world. These countries would be important in their own right to Americans; arguably, after 9/11, they became vital to our national security. And the enduring impact of Islam is a crucial factor we must understand. We at the Foreign Policy Research Institute hope these books will illuminate both the facts and the prospects.

U.S. Navy personnel stand on the deck of the destroyer USS *Cole*, just above a hole caused by a terrorist attack while the ship was entering the port of Aden, Yemen, October 12, 2000. The suicide bombing killed 17 U.S. sailors and injured more than 40 others.

Place in the World

The port of Aden is one of the busiest places in Yemen, a nation that is located along the southern coastline of the Arabian Peninsula. Each year, some 2,000 vessels make their way in and out of the huge natural port. Some of the ships can be seen in any port on Earth; they include cargo-carrying merchant vessels toting coffee, fish, and tobacco, which are among the few goods Yemen exports to other countries. Also, a visitor might see an occasional oil tanker sailing in and out of the port. Yemen has petroleum reserves, but it is hardly in the same class as some of the other countries with which it shares the peninsula, such as Saudi Arabia, the United Arab Emirates, or Kuwait. Those nations are truly oil **sheikhdoms** where petroleum reserves generate billions of dollars a year in revenue. Yemen's supply of oil is much more modest.

Making their way through the harbor among the large

merchant vessels are the much smaller boats piloted by fishermen and others who make their livings in the nearby Red Sea, Gulf of Aden, and Arabian Sea. Many of these boats are dhows—small, wooden fishing boats with a design that hasn't changed much since biblical times. Most of the dhows that sail out of the port of Aden are now powered by gasoline engines rather than sails. The dhows are a testament to Yemen's long history as a seafaring nation. Much of Yemen's success as a seafaring nation owes to its long coastline, which runs nearly 1,200 miles (1,931 kilometers), about the distance from New York City to Miami along the United States' Atlantic coast.

TENSION IN THE MIDDLE EAST

By the fall of 2000, U.S. Navy warships were also becoming common sights in the port of Aden. Throughout the Middle East, tensions were on edge, and the leaders of the United States wanted their forces to be there to address any volatile situation that might arise in the region.

The U.S. and other major world powers were deeply concerned over increasing violence between Palestinian Arabs and Israeli Jews that began in September 2000. For decades, Palestinians had been demanding autonomy for the West Bank, an area of land along the Jordan River, and the Gaza Strip, in southern Israel along the Mediterranean. The Palestinians wanted recognition as an independent state, and during a series of meetings with U.S. president Bill Clinton in the 1990s, a process had been negotiated that, it was hoped, would result in a peaceful resolution of the long-running conflict.

However, at a final summit at Camp David, Maryland, in September 2000 Palestinian leader Yasir Arafat rejected Israel's peace plan. He urged Palestinians to demonstrate against the Israelis. Demonstrations quickly became violent, and by October

Palestinian extremists were waging open warfare on the streets. Israelis began to fear suicide bombers—individuals who would strap high explosives to themselves, then ignite the bombs in crowded places such as buses, restaurants, and shopping centers.

Other parts of the Middle East teetered on the edge of war as well. Hostilities between Iran and the United States have persisted since 1979, when a pro-American government was deposed in favor of a regime headed by *fundamentalist* Muslim clerics. In Iraq, dictator Saddam Hussein had invaded Kuwait in 1990, then

During the 1990s, Islamist groups carried out numerous attacks against U.S. targets in the Middle East. On June 25, 1996, terrorists exploded a fuel truck outside the Khobar Towers, on King Abd al-Aziz Air Base near Dhahran, Saudi Arabia. Khobar Towers housed U.S. soldiers and served as the headquarters for the U.S. Air Force's 4404th Wing. The blast killed 19 American airmen and injured 370 Americans and Saudis.

survived the American-led military force that ousted his soldiers from the **Gulf state**. Although the United Nations had ordered Iraq to disarm, Saddam frustrated the efforts of U.N. weapons inspectors; after the inspectors were withdrawn in 1998, diplomats suspected that Saddam was re-arming his military and planned to strike again. In Saudi Arabia, 19 U.S. Air Force personnel had been killed in 1996 when a terrorist's bomb exploded outside the Khobar Towers housing complex near the city of Dhahran. Two years later, in August 1998, 224 people—including 12 Americans— were killed when suicide bombers drove trucks laden with explosives into U.S. embassy compounds in Kenya and Tanzania in Africa. The chief suspect in the embassy bombings was al-Qaeda, a terrorist group headed by a fugitive Islamic militant from Saudi Arabia named Osama bin Laden.

American officials were particularly concerned about terrorism in Yemen, where a lack of government stability had helped to allow

Ali Abdullah Salih speaks with the press outside the White House after meeting with U.S. president George W. Bush in November 2001. Yemen's government has cooperated with the U.S. during Bush's "war on terrorism."

terrorist groups to operate unchecked. For much of the past two centuries, the country had been divided into two states, most recently known as North Yemen and South Yemen. Leaders of the two states constantly bickered, often engaging in border fights and raids. Meanwhile, the two countries suffered through many civil wars. In 1990 the two Yemens were united into a single country, although a brief civil war broke out afterwards. In 1994, at the war's end, an uneasy peace settled over the country as the Yemenis got down to the business of forging a unified nation. Still, in the rocky wilderness of the Yemen desert, it was believed that many terrorist groups were hiding and making plans for armed assaults on their enemies. Al-Qaeda was among the groups suspected of operating in Yemen.

TRADITION AND MODERN DEVELOPMENTS

Yemen is a poor country, in which many modern manufacturing and agricultural techniques are unknown. Its people have held onto old traditions. Many of them continue to dress in the traditional garments that have been worn by Yemenis for generations; in fact, a curved ceremonial dagger known as the *jambiya* is still carried in the belts of Yemeni men. Many Yemeni women follow strict Islamic dress codes and cover their faces in public. And most men in Yemen gather each afternoon to chew *qat*, a mild stimulant that has become as much a part of the culture in Yemen as chewing gum is in the United States.

But the country has shaken off some traditions and embraced the 21st century. Yemen is one of the few countries in the Arab world in which the people elect their parliament and president. No royal family presides over Yemen, as is the case in Saudi Arabia, Kuwait, Oman, and other nations. The president, Ali Abdullah Salih, was last elected in 2006 and faces election again in 2013. What's more, women have the right to vote as well as hold elective office in Yemen. Such rights for women are rare in many Arab countries.

Shortly after Yemen was unified in 1990, the country found itself estranged from the West because it refused to join an international coalition that forced Iraqi forces to withdraw from Kuwait in 1991. But in recent years, there had been a thaw in relations between Yemen and America. In April 2000, President Salih visited Washington and met with President Bill Clinton. Soon after, Yemen was permitting the U.S. Navy to anchor in the port of Aden, where the ships were refueled.

The United States intended to use the port of Aden as a refueling stop to help revive the economy of Yemen. This, it was hoped, would prove to foreign traders that Aden was safe for merchant ships, and give the government of Yemen a measure of respectability. In return, U.S. leaders hoped that a warming of relations between the two countries would convince the Yemenis to kick out the terrorists and engage in trade with the West. "We were helping Yemen help itself and everyone in the region was interested in having us help them change," explained General Anthony C. Zinni, overall commander of American armed forces in the Middle East.

THE USS COLE DISASTER

When the USS *Cole* sailed into the port of Aden in the morning hours of October 12, 2000, it is likely that few people living in the city took much notice. The *Cole* was the third American warship to drop anchor in the port of Aden since Salih had returned from Washington some five months before.

At the time, the *Cole* was one of the most sophisticated ships in the American fleet. The *Cole* was the length of a football field, equipped with advanced radar systems and armed with high-speed missiles and cannons. Its mission was to accompany other ships into dangerous zones and protect them from attack. In the Persian

Gulf, it had been assigned to the American **contingent** of ships charged with enforcing a trade embargo on Iraq, which had been declared since Saddam ordered his troops to invade Kuwait a decade before. When crews from the *Cole* and other U.S. ships boarded merchant vessels in the Persian Gulf and discovered weapons and other embargoed goods bound for Iraq, the American warships would accompany those ships to nearby harbors where their cargoes were confiscated. Some of those renegade ships had even been unloaded in Aden.

It was a typical morning in Aden when the *Cole* approached the port just before 9 A.M. The hot sun had already raised the

A close-up view of the damaged *Cole*. U.S. officials determined that Abd al-Rahim al-Nashiri, the chief of Persian Gulf operations for the al-Qaeda terrorist network, was responsible for planning the *Cole* attack, as well as other attacks against U.S. targets. Abd al-Rahim was captured in Yemen in November 2002. After the attack the *Cole* was brought back to the United States, where it was repaired; the warship returned to full duty in April 2002.

thermometer to 100°F (38°C). A few days before the *Cole* arrived, navy officers stationed in Aden hired a contractor to meet the *Cole* in the harbor, help it anchor, and provide the ship with fuel. The *Cole* expected to spend no more than a few hours in Aden before continuing on its mission.

About one mile from shore, several small boats hired by the refueling contractor chugged out to meet the *Cole*. The boats swarmed around the *Cole* while American sailors on deck tossed fastening lines to the Arab seamen below. Next, the lines were fastened to buoys in the harbor that were anchored to the sea floor. Once it was secured in a resting position, the *Cole* would remain relatively motionless so that the refueling tanker could dock with the *Cole* and transfer its diesel fuel to the American warship.

While the ship was being anchored, American sailors on deck noticed a small rubber craft dart in and out of the mooring boats. Later, the Americans would say that they believed the rubber craft was one of the mooring boats and that it approached the *Cole* to retrieve a line. Other witnesses would report that the two men aboard the rubber boat stood at attention, as if in military formation, as the craft pulled right alongside the hull of the destroyer.

An instant later the giant ship shook from a tremendous explosion. A bomb had been aboard the rubber boat and the two men who piloted the craft were terrorists—suicide bombers. The explosion blasted a huge hole through the half-inch steel hull of the *Cole*. Later, investigators measured the hole at 80 feet (24 meters) long by 40 feet (12 meters) high. The shockwave burst into the *Cole*'s engine room, mess hall, and kitchen. Water rushed into the ship. Fires erupted throughout the vessel. The force of the explosion bent hatches, collapsed decks, and punched out bulkheads as though they were sheets of paper. Hisham Bashraheel, an editor at an Aden newspaper, reported that the people onshore thought the explosion was an earthquake.

The blast killed 17 crew members aboard the *Cole*. Some of the Americans were as young as 19 years old. They had been in the navy for just a few months and were serving on their maiden voyages. Others killed in the explosion were navy veterans; some planned to leave the service at the conclusion of the *Cole*'s mission.

Within days, some 300 American investigators arrived in Aden to search for clues. The Americans had been dispatched by the Federal Bureau of Investigation (FBI) and Central Intelligence Agency (CIA) as well as by military intelligence agencies. The clues soon pointed to al-Qaeda and Osama bin Laden. President Clinton declared that the United States would retaliate against the planners of the *Cole* bombing. "If, as it now appears, this was an act of terrorism, it was a despicable and cowardly act," Clinton said just a few hours after the bombing. "We will find out who was responsible and hold them accountable."

There would be no immediate retaliation, however. Following the Kenya and Tanzania bombings in 1998, Clinton ordered a cruise-missile strike on a pharmaceutical plant in Sudan after the CIA reported that it was secretly manufacturing chemical weapons for use by al-Qaeda. Later, evidence suggested that the CIA was wrong, and that the plant was a legitimate drug manufacturer. Clearly, after the attack on the *Cole*, Clinton thought it was prudent to use caution before striking back against al-Qaeda.

And so, Osama bin Laden and the other terrorists remained well beyond the reach of the Americans. They had found refuge in Afghanistan, where they planned a much more devastating attack on the United States—the September 11, 2001, airline hijackings and suicide attacks on the World Trade Center in New York and the Pentagon in Washington, in which nearly 3,000 people were killed.

For Americans who wondered how their country could have been caught by surprise by such a vicious act of terrorism, they need only have looked to Yemen for the first clue.

Women walk down an ancient stone staircase to collect water for cooking and drinking. Water is an important commodity in this desert land.

The Land

During the 1880s, the French poet Arthur Rimbaud left his homeland. After he arrived in Yemen he tried to make a living first by trading coffee, then at the more dangerous business of selling guns to the Arab tribes of the mountains and deserts. While Rimbaud was living in the region, much of the southern portion of the country was known as Aden, a name today reserved for just the port city. Here is how Rimbaud described the climate in a letter he wrote to his family back home:

> Aden is a horrible rock, without a single blade of grass or a drop of fresh water: we drink distilled sea water. The heat is extreme, especially in June and September, which are the dog days here. The constant temperature, night and day, in a very cool and well-ventilated office, is 95 degrees. . . . I'm like a prisoner here. . . .

Today, parts of Yemen are not much different than they were in Rimbaud's time more than a century ago.

CLIMATE

Although many of the coastal plains are as hot and humid as Aden, there are also temperate regions in the country and awe-inspiring mountains where it is cool in the summer and cold in the winter. Most of Yemen's farming takes places in these highland areas where the rainfall is somewhat higher and the mountain slopes are covered with numerous, narrow terraces. In addition to vegetables and fruits such as grapes, Yemen is famous for growing coffee, as well as *qat*, which competes with coffee for land and the country's water supply.

Sandstorms plague inland desert areas of the country. There is little native wildlife, and the country has its share of ecological problems. Few laws govern waste disposal, so it is not unusual for a visitor to see bags of trash and garbage tossed helter-skelter into the countryside.

Yemen is located just 400 miles (644 km) south of the ***tropic of***

A satellite view of the Bab el Mandeb, showing the Yemen area. The Bab el Mandeb (Strait of Mandeb) is a strategic chokepoint for the world's oil supply; if it were closed, tankers would not be able to reach the Suez Canal and the Sumed Pipeline complex. Instead, they would have to travel south around Africa, which would greatly extend the time needed for the oil to reach the West.

Yemen is more mountainous than many other countries of the Persian Gulf region. The lowlands, which run in a narrow band along the coast, rise to mountains in the interior of the country. The highest point is Jabal (or Mount) an Nabi Shu'ayb, which is about 12,336 feet (3,760 meters) high.

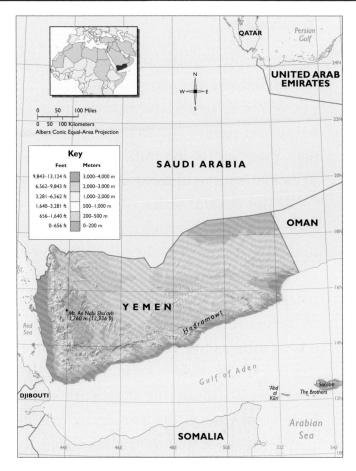

Cancer, which is a primary factor behind the oppressiveness of the heat. The regions on Earth that receive the most direct sunlight fall between the lines of latitude known as the tropic of Cancer, in the northern hemisphere, and the **tropic of Capricorn**, in the southern hemisphere. The tropics lie 23.5 degrees above and below the **equator**. The region between the two tropics is known as the Torrid Zone.

There is more than just direct sunlight affecting the arid climate. Gigantic air swirls are created by the revolution of the earth. These air swirls lose heat as they reach the upper atmosphere, then rise in temperature again as they descend on the Torrid Zone. This constant barrage of sunlight and hot air has dried out the region's soil.

TOPOGRAPHY

Since much of the soil can't hold water, agriculture is difficult in the highlands and virtually nothing can grow in the desert. Just 3 percent of Yemen's land is in farmland regions. The main crops are fruits, vegetables, grains, coffee, cotton, and *qat*. Yemeni farmers also raise cattle for milk and beef, but goats and sheep are the principal source of meat and other products.

In the coastal areas of Yemen, the climate is dry and hot with little rainfall. Average annual rainfall in the coastal regions amounts to just 9 inches (23 centimeters) a year, and some areas along the coast receive less. The port city of Aden, for example, receives just 5 inches (12.7 cm) of rainfall a year. In some sections of the country, it is not uncommon for there to be no rain for periods as long as five years. Because there is so little rain and because the terrain is mostly sandy, winds sweeping through the country occasionally cause blinding sandstorms. Heavy windstorms that blow across the entire peninsula are known as *shammals*.

Yemen is located at the southern tip of the Arabian Peninsula, south of Saudi Arabia and west of Oman. It is roughly the size of France. All of Yemen's territory is land; there are no inland lakes or rivers. The country's long coastline borders the Red Sea to the west and the Gulf of Aden to the south. Beyond the Gulf of Aden lies the Arabian Sea and Indian Ocean.

Separating the Gulf of Aden from the Red Sea is a narrow strait known as the Bab el Mandeb, an Arabic name that means "Gate of Tears." Just 17 miles (27 km) across the strait is the continent of Africa. Yemen's closest African neighbors are the nations of Eritrea, Djibouti, and Somalia. Several islands in the Red Sea and Gulf of Aden are claimed by Yemen. The largest island is Socotra, which is in the Gulf of Aden. Another island is Kamaran, just off the western coast in the Red Sea. For decades, the British maintained a *quarantine* station on Kamaran for Muslims making their annual pilgrimage to Mecca in Saudi Arabia, but when the British left in 1967 the island reverted to Yemen's control. Another small island under Yemen's ownership is Perim, which is in the Bab el Mandeb.

THE HIGHLANDS

The highest peaks in Yemen, which are also the highest peaks anywhere on the Arabian Peninsula, can be found in a range of highlands that run along the western coasts of Yemen and into

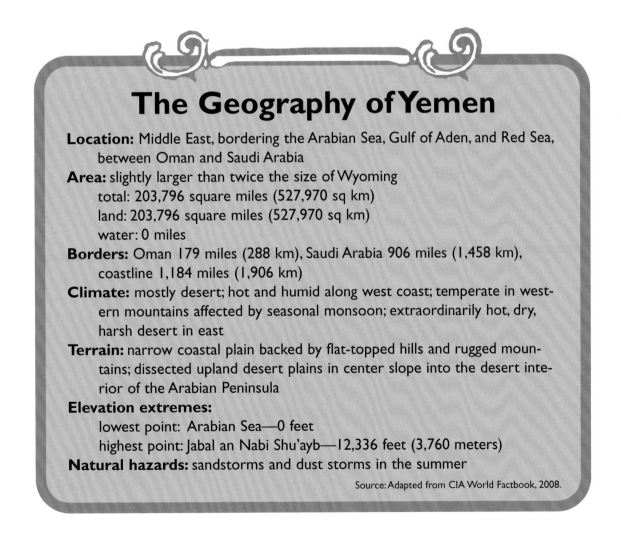

The Geography of Yemen

Location: Middle East, bordering the Arabian Sea, Gulf of Aden, and Red Sea, between Oman and Saudi Arabia

Area: slightly larger than twice the size of Wyoming
total: 203,796 square miles (527,970 sq km)
land: 203,796 square miles (527,970 sq km)
water: 0 miles

Borders: Oman 179 miles (288 km), Saudi Arabia 906 miles (1,458 km), coastline 1,184 miles (1,906 km)

Climate: mostly desert; hot and humid along west coast; temperate in western mountains affected by seasonal monsoon; extraordinarily hot, dry, harsh desert in east

Terrain: narrow coastal plain backed by flat-topped hills and rugged mountains; dissected upland desert plains in center slope into the desert interior of the Arabian Peninsula

Elevation extremes:
lowest point: Arabian Sea—0 feet
highest point: Jabal an Nabi Shu'ayb—12,336 feet (3,760 meters)

Natural hazards: sandstorms and dust storms in the summer

Source: Adapted from CIA World Factbook, 2008.

Saudi Arabia. Sanaa, Yemen's capital, sits in a flat plain among the western highlands at an elevation of 7,380 feet (2,249 meters), which is more than a mile high. Because the tallest mountains on the peninsula are found in Yemen, the country is nicknamed the "Roof of Arabia."

From the western highlands, the geography of the peninsula slopes down toward the east, ending at sea level along the coasts of Oman, the United Arab Emirates, Qatar, Saudi Arabia, and Kuwait. The western mountains back up to the Red Sea but there is a narrow coastal strip of land known as the Tihama, which extends from the southernmost tip of Yemen along the Gulf of Aden north into Saudi Arabia.

To the south, the western highlands follow the coast and make a sharp turn toward the east, running parallel to Yemen's southern coastline to the country's border with Oman. The mountains here aren't quite as high as they are in the west. By the time they cross the Oman border, the elevation of the terrain is about 3,200 feet (975 meters) above sea level.

There is one final range of mountains in Yemen—a smaller range that emerges from the western highlands and runs eastward along the northern border of the country. The oil reserves that have been recently discovered in Yemen can be found at the southern ridge of this range.

Throughout the mountains, travelers can find green valleys where the heat takes a break and vegetation is able to grow. These valleys are known as the wadis. The largest and most fertile valley in Yemen is the Wadi Hadhramaut, located in the southern mountain range. Although it is a place of cultivable soil and inhabited by a population of farmers, there is no question that the wadi is surrounded by a bleak, craggy landscape. Perhaps that is why ancient travelers named the wadi *Hadhramaut*, which is sometimes said to derive from the Arabic for "death is present."

The mountains themselves can be hazardous. Along with the obvious dangers one would encounter while traveling along ancient and dusty roadways in rocky terrain where bandits, kidnappers, and terrorists are believed to be hiding, the mountains themselves often cause trouble. Some of the peaks are volcanically active. Hot springs deep underground occasionally cause earthquakes. In 1982, an earthquake rocked the region of Dharma in the western highlands, killing some 2,500 people. It was the largest natural catastrophe in Yemen's history.

Clouds dot the sky over an old palace built of mud brick in the Wadi Hadhramaut. This is one of the fertile areas of Yemen.

The Island of Bliss

Just 200 miles (322 km) south of the Yemen mainland lies the island of Socotra. The island, which is about 93 miles (150 km) long and 23 miles (37 km) wide, is Yemen's largest island. It is located beyond the Gulf of Aden in the Indian Ocean.

Socotra is unlike the mainland, especially in its appearance. While Yemen is dominated by rocky and rugged terrain as well as sandy deserts, Socotra features all manner of animals and lush plants, which have fascinated visitors for centuries. But the people of Socotra are similar to the mainlanders in that they have known few modern conveniences.

When the British arrived in the 1940s to establish a military base during World War II, they discovered that the last map of Socotra had been drawn in 1835. Following the war, expeditions were dispatched by Great Britain's Royal Geographic Society to explore the island. Written accounts show that the expedition leaders took note of the island's mud and coral houses, its small tobacco plantations, and its unique breed of dwarf cows.

One famous visitor to the island was Marco Polo, the merchant and explorer. He stopped in Socotra on his way home from China in the 13th century. The island, Polo wrote,

> abounds with the necessaries of life. The inhabitants find much ambergris [a fluid that is used as a perfume ingredient] upon their coasts, which is voided from the entrails of whales. Being an article of merchandise in great demand, they make it a business to take these fish; and this they do by means of a barbed iron, which they strike into the whale so firmly that it cannot be drawn out. To the iron a long line is fastened, with a buoy at the end, for the purpose of discovering the place where the fish, when dead, is to be found. They then drag it to the shore, and proceed to extract the ambergris from its belly, whilst from its head they procure several casks of oil.

Over the years, there has never been agreement on how Socotra earned its name. Some Arabic scholars have guessed the original name to be *Suq Qatr*, which means "Emporium of Resin." For centuries, incense traders found trees in Yemen as well as Socotra that produced the resin frankincense, which was a highly valued ingredient of perfume.

Greek sailors called the island *Dioskurida*. In Sanskrit, an ancient language of India, the term *Dvipa Sakhadara* means "Island of Bliss." This could be yet another source of the island's name.

North of the southern highlands, the rocky terrain slopes down and turns into the vast Arabian desert. In Arabic, the name of the desert is the *Ar-Rub al-Khali*, which means "Empty Quarter."

Maximum daytime temperatures in the coastal regions range from 89°F (32°C) in the winter months to 104°F (40°C) in the summertime. It is also very humid in this region. Many visitors complain of the stifling air, especially in the months between May and October, which are further plagued by sandstorms.

The country's highlands offer a break from the heat. Temperatures range from highs of 71°F (22°C) in June, the warmest month, to 57°F (14°C) in January, the coldest time of the year in Yemen. It rains much more in the mountains than it does along the coast. Residents of the mountainous regions may see as much as 30 inches (76.2 cm) of rain a year. The fertile wadis receive rainfall in short, heavy showers that fall mostly in April, June, August, and September. At other times, the climate in the wadis is arid and hot. Crops are often damaged by sandstorms.

AGRICULTURE

Yemen is a case study in how a country should not manage its water resources. More than 3,000 species of plants can be found in Yemen, but only about 300 of them are endemic, meaning they are native to the country. Over the years, poor agricultural techniques practiced by Yemeni farmers have caused erosion and robbed the land of its topsoil. Overgrazing by cattle and sheep has also stripped the land of the native grasses that held the topsoil in place. With no grasses to anchor the soil, the heavy winds common to the region blew most of the good soil away. Rainwater washed away much of the remaining soil. In the 1970s and 1980s, the oil boom lured many Yemeni farmers to better-paying jobs in the oilfields of Saudi Arabia, Kuwait, and other Gulf states. The farmers left behind their fields, and with no one to till them they soon became

A grove of dragon's blood trees on Socotra Island, Yemen.

fallow. This negligence led to even further erosion.

Making the agricultural situation worse in Yemen is the rapid population growth during the past three decades. The rising birth rate has meant that more people have relied on soil that was scarce to begin with. In many of the wadis, a local official known as the *muqassim ad-dayi* (divider of the water) has been appointed. Mushin Ataya, the *muqassim ad-dayi* in the Wadi Dahr, explained his job to a reporter: "We have water but it is precious. My job is to see that not a drop is wasted and that it is fairly shared."

WILDLIFE

Animals are not common sights in Yemen. Most live in the mountains. They include the mountain gazelle, baboon, red fox, sand fox, striped hyena, Arabian wolf, jackal, Arabian leopard, and ibex, which is a long-horned wild goat. There are more than 360 species of birds in Yemen. They primarily live in the mountains, where many snakes and lizards also live. Common snakes found among the rocky crags are cobras and vipers. Geckos, chameleons, and other tiny lizards also make their homes among the rocks.

The desert isn't totally devoid of wildlife. There are plenty of flies and mosquitoes to swat as well as scorpions underfoot. There are more than 100 species of butterflies recorded in the country as well. Swarms of locusts are often blown across the Red Sea from Africa. Yemenis enjoy eating these insects roasted!

Yemen also has camels, though they are not as common a sight there as they are in other Arab lands. Unlike the citizens of those countries, the Yemenis are generally not nomadic. Therefore, they have little use for camels, which are able to transport their riders and carry loads across long miles of blazing desert with very little drinking water.

MODERN DEVELOPMENTS

For several decades, Yemen existed as a state where modern products, communications, and science were unknown. To compensate for a lack of technology, Yemenis wasted nothing—even human excrement was collected and burned for fuel; then, the ashes were sold to farmers as fertilizer.

During the 1990s, Yemen underwent a few modern developments. Yemenis began welcoming Western tourists and their respective cultures. The arrival of visitors and traders, however, also introduced to Yemen the synthetic materials common to American and European cities—plastic bags, paper products, disposable diapers, and dozens of other kinds of refuse. In many developed nations, such refuse goes into sanitary landfills, recycling centers, incinerators, and trash-to-energy plants. For years, Yemenis did not make trash disposal a priority. Now inundated with trash, the country is forced to figure out what to do with it all.

Detail from the painting "Solomon and the Queen of Sheba," by the 17th-century artist Eustache Lesueur, which depicts the famous meeting described in the Bible. Since ancient times Yemen has been the location of human civilizations.

History

Sometime between 950 and 930 B.C., a famous meeting took place in Jerusalem, according to the Biblical book of Second Chronicles. The Israelite king Solomon was visited by a distinguished foreigner named Bilqis, the ruler of the land in southern Arabia known as Saba, which has been translated into "Sheba." Solomon ruled the land north of Saba that is Israel today.

The Bible says, "And when the Queen of Sheba heard of the fame of Solomon, she came to prove Solomon with hard questions at Jerusalem, with a very great company, and camels that bare spices, and gold in abundance, and precious stones: and when she was come to Solomon, she communed with him of all that was in her heart. . . . And King Solomon gave to the Queen of Sheba all her desire, whatsoever she asked. . . . So she turned, and went away to her own land, she and her servants." (2 Chron., 9: 1, 12)

Solomon had a powerful army and Bilqis wanted assurances that he would not use it to disrupt Saba's valuable trade in frankincense and myrrh. Those were the "hard questions" she posed to Solomon. According to passages in the Bible, the two monarchs hit it off, lavished gifts on one another, and Bilqis went home happy.

During the reign of the Queen of Sheba, the country that is now Yemen dominated trade, fielded a powerful army, and made contributions in engineering and architecture that were centuries ahead of their time. During the rule of the Romans about 1,000 years later the region was known as *Arabia Felix*, a Latin term that means "Happy Arabia." But in recent years, Yemen has suffered through long periods of conquest, poverty, and civil war. In contemporary times Yemen has been anything but a happy place.

YEMEN'S ANCIENT PAST

Many Yemenis believe their country may be the oldest established civilization on Earth. According to legend, the Yemen capital of Sanaa was founded by Shem, a son of Noah. Following the great flood that is said to have cleansed the world of its sins, the Noah's ark made its landing in the mountains of Ararat, which is in Turkey. Yemenis believe Shem made his way south into Arabia and, after following the path of a bird sent by Allah (God), he founded a city on a plain at the foot of Mount Nugum. He called the city *Madinat Sam*, which means "city of Shem." Eventually, the name was changed to *Sanaa*, "Fortified One." Shem is believed to be the first of the Semites, the ancestors of the Jews and Arabs.

Science has provided its own evidence about Yemen's ancient past. Archaeological digs have uncovered remnants of Stone Age tools in the mountains near the Bab el Mandeb, indicating cave dwellers lived in Yemen some 40,000 years ago. Also, excavations in some of the wadis have uncovered fossils of a prehistoric crocodile dating back 165 million years.

The terrain along the southern Arabian coast was rich in balsam trees that produced the resin frankincense and herbs that produced myrrh, both highly valued ingredients of perfume. The scents had other uses as well: some cultures found a medicinal use for frankincense, and Jews burned frankincense and myrrh during religious rituals. Many cultures used them in funeral rites. In Egypt, the mummies of the royal family were scented with

The ruins of Diga are located near Marib, Yemen. These ancient remains date back to the seventh century B.C.

frankincense and myrrh before they were entombed. The Gospels of the New Testament say that when the wise men visited the baby Jesus, among the gifts bestowed on the child were frankincense, myrrh, and "the gold of Sheba."

THE KINGDOM OF SABA

And so kingdoms grew along the trade routes of southern Arabia. Ports were established in the coastal areas, where frankincense and myrrh could be shipped abroad. Spices and pearls were soon added to cargoes along the trade routes as well. By the year 1000 B.C., the most powerful kingdom in southern Arabia was Saba, which established its capital at Marib at the foot of the western highlands in the country's interior. Marib is said to have had a population as large as 300,000. Remnants from the old capital remain standing today.

Historians believe that the people of Saba were quite advanced. They erected buildings that were several stories high during a time when the people of North America were living in huts and caves. They constructed a great dam near Marib, some 2,000 feet (609 meters) across, that caught the rain draining from the wadis and provided irrigation for 4,000 acres of cropland. The dam was erected around 500 B.C. and stood for a thousand years before collapsing.

THE HIMYARITES

The Sabaean empire's total control of southern Arabia ended around 300 B.C. Other kingdoms, such as the Hadhramaut and Qataban, grew in strength and challenged Saba's dominance of the trade routes. The kingdoms fought among each other for control. Around A.D. 300, a tribe known as the Himyarites emerged as the dominant people of southern Arabia. In the 20th century, political leaders in North Yemen claimed descent from the Himyarites.

In A.D. 323, the Roman emperor Constantine declared

Christianity the religion of the Roman Empire. Christians did not use frankincense and myrrh in their ceremonies. As a result, there was no longer a great demand for the fragrances, and trade in the region faced setbacks. Meanwhile, the Himyarites had to ward off aggressors from other lands. During the fourth century the Ethiopians crossed the Bab el Mandeb and conquered southern Arabia, ruling for 40 years. Eventually, the Himyarites regained power and kicked the Ethiopians out of the country. Jews had resided in parts of the Arabian Peninsula, and one converted Jew, Yusuf Asar, briefly ruled the Himyarite kingdom. There also were Christians who established their religion in southern Arabia.

By 570, Christianity was the dominant religion in southern Arabia. That was the year the dam at Marib collapsed, forcing the citizens of the former Sabaean capital to migrate to other settlements throughout the southern region of the peninsula. It was also an important year because Abraha, a Christian ruler, was ousted from the throne by a group of Himyarites who sought to regain power. The year is known as the "year of the elephant" because Abraha is said to have driven a herd of elephants north to attack the Arabian city of Mecca.

The Himyarites were able to defeat Abraha, but they never regained power because they were forced to enlist the Persians as allies. Once Abraha was expelled, the Persians stayed and within five years they were in control of the south.

THE RISE AND SPREAD OF ISLAM

While the Himyarites bristled under the rule of the Persians, events unfolding elsewhere on the Arabian Peninsula would soon have an impact on the south. In 570, a man named Muhammad was born in Mecca, a city in what today is Saudi Arabia. Some 40 years later, Muhammad began to receive divine messages that there was just one god, Allah. Muhammad was told to spread this

Saladin (1138–1193) was the greatest Muslim leader during the period of the Crusades. In 1187 he recaptured Jerusalem from the Christian Crusaders, who had taken control of the city in 1099. Saladin had become the ruler of Egypt in 1171, and was the most powerful Muslim leader within a few years. He sent his brother to rule over the region that today is Yemen in 1173.

message to the polytheistic people of the Arabian Peninsula. His efforts to do Allah's will gave birth to a new religion, Islam.

At first, Arabs in Mecca and elsewhere refused to accept the new religion. Many of them worshiped multiple deities and rejected the idea of worshiping one supreme being. Slowly, however, the Arab people began converting. Most of the early followers were drawn to Islam by the personal appeal of Muhammad, a persuasive and charismatic leader who possessed a gift for resolving disputes. Others joined Islam after they were conquered by Muhammad's armies. Unlike the first Christians, who had been taught to turn the other cheek, the Muslims were prepared to fight to spread the word of the Prophet.

No such force was needed in southern Arabia. In 628, Badhan, the Persian governor of southern Arabia, converted to Islam. Soon, almost everyone else living in the country had joined the new faith. Around this time Yemen received its modern name: in Arabic, Yemen means "the right side," the position the country occupies on the peninsula when one faces east from Mecca.

In 632, the much-beloved Prophet Muhammad died. The new Islamic leader was Abu Bakr, who was elected by the Muslim community as the first caliph. Under Abu Bakr the Muslims became a formidable military force and their influence spread throughout the Arab world.

As the religion of Islam spread and grew, so did the Middle East itself. The great Middle East cities of Damascus, Alexandria, Beirut, Jerusalem, Amman, Baghdad, and Cairo became important trading centers. For some 200 years, the Christian armies of Western Europe battled with the Muslim forces over Jerusalem and other sites holy to Christianity. The first of the Crusades began in 1095; they ended in failure in 1291, when the Christians were killed or forced from their strongholds on the coast. The most fearsome Muslim warrior during the period of the Crusades was Saladin, the sultan of Egypt, whose empire stretched from the Libyan desert in North Africa to the Tigris River in Iraq.

THE ZAYDI DYNASTY

In the late seventh century, a split developed in the Islamic world between Shiite and Sunni Muslims. They two groups maintained different interpretations of who the legitimate caliph should be.

Zayd ibn Ali Zayn al-Abidin, a Shiite and great-great-grandson of the Prophet, led a rebellion against the Sunnis in southern Arabia. He was killed in 740, but his descendants, called Zaydis, fought the Sunnis for power. By the end of the ninth century, the Zaydis were in control of the region that would become North

Yemen. The imam, or leader, of the community was al-Hadi ila al-Haqq. Although Zaydi influence would rise and fall over the years—at times throughout history the Zaydis would control very little territory—Zaydi imams would maintain some degree of power in Yemen until 1962.

The Zaydis constantly had to fend off challenges from other groups, such as the Ismailis, Mahdis, Tahirids, and Shafiis. Over the years, the rulers of these sects and others would claim power in Yemen. Some of the ruling families remained in power for hundreds of years while others managed to hold their thrones for just brief periods. The city of Sanaa, for example, fell under 20 different rulers over the course of the first 12 years of the 10th century. Attempts to unify the people of the region rarely succeeded. In 1063, an Ismaili ruler named Ali al-Sulayhi forged a unified kingdom, but he was murdered and his chronically ill son, al-Mukarram Ahmad, decided to pass the throne to his wife, Queen Arwa. She was unable to hold the kingdom together and died in 1138.

In 1173 Saladin dispatched his brother to rule southern Arabia. Saladin's dynastic family, the Ayyubids, stayed in power for some 200 years, but by the mid-1300s the Zaydis were raiding cities in Yemen and Ayyubid rule broke down. In the 1500s, the Zaydis were back in power. However, they often found themselves repelling attacks by Egyptian invaders.

THE OTTOMANS IN YEMEN

During the 14th century, north of the Arabian Peninsula in Turkey, a warlord named Osman established the foundations of what would become the Ottoman Empire. The Ottoman Turks would prove to be one of the most formidable military dynasties in the history of the world, expanding their realm west into Europe and, by the 16th century, south into Arabia.

The Ottoman Turks arrived in Yemen in 1538. They installed a

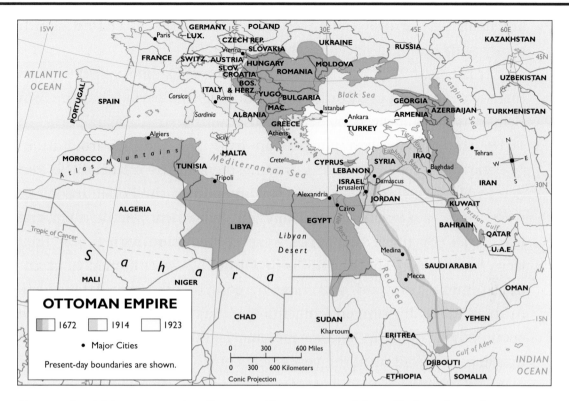

During the 16th century, the Ottoman Empire spread from Turkey throughout the Middle East; the Yemen region came under its control around 1538. By 1672 the empire controlled the Middle East, as well as large parts of north Africa, central Asia, and eastern Europe. By the 18th and 19th centuries, however, although the Ottomans claimed to control the region, the British were in fact the major imperial power in the Persian Gulf. By the beginning of World War I (1914), the Ottoman Empire was concentrated in the Middle East, and after the war Ottoman territories were divided among the victorious allied powers.

pasha, or governor, and ruled over the three great cities of southern Arabia: Aden, Sanaa, and Taizz. The Turkish rule was cruel and brutal and the Zaydis seethed under the Ottoman domination. In 1590, a 20-year-old Zaydi leader named al-Mansur Billah al-Qasim organized a resistance against the Turks. For years, the Turks hunted al-Qasim across the mountains and deserts of Yemen, but the young rebel proved to be an effective **guerrilla** fighter and managed to elude the invaders. By 1608, al-Qasim was so powerful that the Turks were forced to sign a treaty with him and agree to share power.

For the next 21 years, the Zaydis under al-Qasim maintained an uneasy peace with the Turks. It was during this period that the first British traders arrived by ship in the southern Arabian ports. In 1618, the British won permission from the Ottoman sultan in Constantinople to establish a trading post on the coast of the Red Sea in Mocha, which was an important port in the coffee trade.

In 1629, al-Qasim's son, Muayyad, led a new rebellion against the Turks. By then, the Turks were preoccupied with a war they were fighting in Italy. In 1637, the Ottomans were forced to abandon Yemen. Muayyad was now in control of most of southern Arabia; his realm ranged from the Red Sea east to the region now occupied by Oman, a distance of some 1,200 miles (1,931 km). This kingdom endured until the years between 1728 and 1731, when the al-Abdali family stole power away from the Zaydi dynasty, and Yemen became divided once again. After the kingdom ruled by Muayyad fell apart, Yemen would not be reunited under a single government until 1990.

By the early part of the 18th century the southern Arabian empire was too vast for the Zaydi imams to control. Aden and the nearby city of Lahij became independent of Zaydi rule. Over the next 100 years the Zaydis lost authority over the entire region east of Aden, while in the north, the Yemenis found themselves threatened by the Wahhabis, a particularly strict sect of Sunni Islam that eventually produced the Al Saud, the current rulers of Saudi Arabia.

In 1798, under the leadership of Napoleon Bonaparte, the French army overthrew the ruling sultans of Egypt, who had been installed by the Ottoman Turks. Suddenly, southern Arabia became a very strategic corner of the world. With France now in control of Egypt at the northern end of the Red Sea, England worried that its longtime enemy would control the sea-lanes between the Middle East and India, which England ruled as a colony. The British quickly established a naval base on the island of Perim in the Bab el Mandeb. Later, they moved the base to Aden and established a hospital in Mocha. The Ottomans were able to force the French out of Egypt in 1801, but the British did not feel threatened to leave Aden.

In 1803, the Wahhabis attacked Yemen and laid siege to Sanaa. Fighting continued for 15 years until the Zaydis made a pact with Muhammad Ali, a maverick Ottoman pasha of Egypt, who dispatched an army to drive off the Wahhabis and re-establish a Zaydi ruler as imam. The Zaydis should have remembered the mistake made by the Himyarites 1,200 years earlier when they couldn't get rid of the Persians after enlisting their help to drive off Abraha. Now, the Zaydis found that the Ottomans intended to stay. In 1833, Muhammad Ali sent his son, a ruthless commander named Ibrahim Pasha, to take Mocha.

THE COLONIAL RULE OF GREAT BRITAIN

Meanwhile, the British had become more of a presence in southern Arabia. To protect their interests, during the 1820s the British signed treaties with local tribes that identified Britain as the dominant foreign power in the Persian Gulf. They also were increasingly concerned about their European rival countries, as well as the Ottoman Empire, vying for control of India and trade routes passing through the region. By the 1830s, steam engines had replaced sails aboard many merchant ships, and the British were in desperate need of a port in southern Arabia where the ships could take on coal. It became clear to the British government that it was in its best economic interest to seize control of the region. In January 1837, the British found the justification they needed to attack the Ottomans in southern Arabia. An Indian ship flying the British flag went aground just off the coast of Aden.

Yemeni pirates soon fell on the ship and plundered it, stealing the possessions of the wealthy Indian passengers. They also threatened to kidnap the Indian women and sell them into slavery.

A British warship under Commander Stafford Bettesworth Haines was dispatched from India with orders to seize Aden from Ahmad ibn Abd al-Karim, the sultan of Lahij, who held power over the port city. When Haines arrived he determined his force was too small to take the city; he offered instead to buy Aden from Ahmad. The two leaders attempted negotiations, but never seemed to make progress. Soon, two more British ships joined Haines's ship off the coast. They carried more than 700 soldiers. Finally, on January 16, 1839, Haines attacked Aden. The British soldiers easily overran the Arab defenders; hundreds of Arabs died in the fighting while the British suffered just 16 casualties.

Haines remained in Aden and became its governor. By the time he left in 1854, the town had grown from a miserable little village of 500 inhabitants to a bustling port city of some 20,000 people. The British eventually took a lot more than just the port city. In time, the British established the Aden Protectorates—a region in the south that would stretch from the Bab el Mandeb to the Oman border. The British remained until 1967 in what eventually became known as South Yemen.

In the north, the Zaydis were dominated by Muhammad Ali's troops, but the pasha had problems of his own. In Constantinople, the Ottoman sultans had demanded that Muhammad Ali show them loyalty and heed their orders. For years he refused, but by 1840 Muhammad Ali was again under their control. After he withdrew his army from southern Arabia, on orders from the Ottoman sultan in Turkey, chaos reigned in northern Yemen. During the next 10 years many tribal leaders made bids for power. The British refused to get involved in the turmoil and bloodshed, and in 1849 the Ottomans established a puppet imam in northern Yemen who ruled with the power of the Turkish army behind him. There were several rebellions during this era, but the Ottomans were able to hold onto power despite the many wars they were forced to fight elsewhere in their realm. The Turks remained in northern Yemen until 1919. By then, their empire had crumbled and was about to be dissolved by the treaties that ended World War I.

IMAM YAHYA

When the Yemenis took back control of their country, it was vastly smaller than the southern Arabian empire that had once been ruled by the Sabaeans and the Himyarites. The Al Saud had seized the northern territory while the British controlled virtually all of the southern. What's more, many tribal sheikhs occupied territory within the country and refused to take orders from a central government. The imam of Yemen during this period was a Zaydi named Yahya bin Muhammad Hamid al-Din. Yahya planned to retake from the Saudis the territory he thought belonged to Yemen.

The imam attacked the Tihama coastal strip first, overrunning hostile sheikhs. Yahya's soldiers were led by his son Ahmad, who would eventually succeed Yahya as ruler of Yemen. By 1926, Yahya signed treaties with Italy and the Soviet Union, two nations hostile to Great Britain. The British, angered by the agreement, ordered air raids on Yemeni positions in the Aden Protectorates. Yahya, convinced now that he could not defeat the powerful British army and worried that he would eventually need his entire military to defend against the Saudis, finally agreed to negotiate a treaty with the British. The pact was signed in 1934, and it guaranteed friendship and mutual cooperation between the Yemenis and British for the next 40 years. It also meant that North Yemen and South Yemen officially became separate states. The pact brought hostilities with the British to an end, but it also pushed back a potential unification between the south and the north.

Nevertheless, Yahya accepted the terms of the 1934 pact and now turned his attention to the north, where, since the uprooting of the Turks, the Al Saud had occupied the northern Tihama coastal plain and western highlands regions known as Asir and Najran. In 1934, a short war broke out between the Yemenis and the Saudis. At the war's conclusion, the Saudis recognized some of the Yemenis' land claims: they withdrew from the coastal plain but refused to leave Asir and Najran. The Treaty of Taif, signed in May

Dar al-Hajar (the Palace of the Rock) was built as a summer home for Imam Yahya during the 1930s. It is located in the fertile valley of Wadi Dahr. Imam Yahya strengthened southern Yemen, fighting at various times against the British and the Saudis.

1934, established the western highlands border between Saudi Arabia and Yemen below Asir.

REVOLUTION IN THE NORTH

Following World War II, a rebellious group known as al-Ahrar al-Yemeniyin—in English, the "Free Yemenis"—made it clear that it intended to topple Yahya. They believed he was too **autocratic**: he meddled too much with private commerce and he was unwilling to modernize Yemen. The Free Yemenis struck in 1948, assassinating the 80-year-old imam in an ambush of his motorcade. The civil war that broke out pitted Yahya's son Ahmad against the Free Yemenis, who had as an ally Sayyid Abdullah al-Wazir, a descendant from a line of imams.

Bloody fighting continued for about a month, with Ahmad emerging victorious. He became imam and—mindful of those complaints against his father that were raised during the **coup** attempt—committed himself to modernizing his country and expanding North Yemen's relations. Yahya had been suspicious of foreigners and accepted no aid from other countries, but Ahmad was eager to make friends with powerful allies. He accepted aid from the United States and Germany. During Ahmad's rein, the Soviets built a modern port in the city of Al Hudayda on the Red Sea, and China built a highway from Al Hudayda to Sanaa.

But Ahmad remained hostile to the British, who continued to administer the Aden Protectorates. In 1953, the British announced plans to create self-rule in Aden. Instead of permitting rule by a Zaydi imam, however, the British proposed an elected council and governor.

Ahmad scoffed at the British proposal, and commenced a guerrilla war against the British, sponsoring the rebellious tribes in the Aden Protectorates to commit terrorism. Meanwhile, Ahmad's problems continued at home. In 1955, army officers plotted a coup and enlisted Ahmad's brother Abdullah among the ranks of the conspirators. Ahmad managed to put down the coup, and then had Abdullah executed.

NASSER STEPS IN

With the conspirators out of the way, Ahmad turned his attention back to the British. In 1956, Ahmad met with two other Arab leaders—King Saud of Saudi Arabia and President Gamal Abdel Nasser of Egypt—and signed the Jidda Pact. The pact, which was negotiated in the Saudi city of Jidda, committed each of the three signing members to the protection of the others in the event of attack by a hostile army. Unknown to Saud and Ahmad, though, Nasser hoped to annex Yemen into a vast Arab republic headed by Egypt. Nasser regarded Yemen's commitment in the Jidda Pact as significant toward his eventual goal of a single Arab state, yet he also had dreams of expanding his authority on the Arabian Peninsula. In 1958, Nasser signed a pact with Syria creating the United Arab Republic. Nasser would soon try to draw Jordan and Iraq into this alliance, which had as one of its goals the destruction of Israel.

The Yemeni army was soon supplied with weapons from the Soviet Union as well as instructors from Egypt. As Yemen continued to build up its military, the British followed through with their plans to create a democracy in the Aden Protectorates. In 1959, a constitution was written for what would be called the Federation of South Arabia, which included the former British colony along with a number of other sheikhdoms and sultanates. Meanwhile, work commenced on the headquarters for the new government. The British made plans to turn the country over to the new government in January 1963 with total independence granted by 1969.

On September 19, 1962, Ahmad died in his sleep from lead poisoning. The imam had never endeared himself to his people. In fact, among Yemenis, Ahmad was known as the "Old Devil." He kept a **harem** of 100 women, was addicted to morphine, and was alleged to have said of Yemen's citizens, "In time of trouble, chop off heads."

Months earlier, Ahmad survived another assassination attempt but the bullets that remained in his body contributed to his final illness. His successor was his son, Muhammad al-Badr, who would rule for just one week. On the night of September 26, a group of dissident army officers led by Colonel Abdullah al-Sallal staged a coup with the blessing, and backing, of Egypt's Nasser. Al-Sallal's men bombarded the palace in Sanaa with cannon fire, and although al-Badr managed to escape into the mountains, the dissidents had

British troops prepare for firing drills with their water-cooled Vickers machine guns at their base near Aden, circa 1957. The British established control over the southern part of Yemen in the mid-19th century, and remained a major influence on the region until 1967.

enough of the army on their side to take control of the government. They declared the end of royal rule and the establishment of the Yemen Arab Republic (YAR). Al-Sallal assumed the presidency, while Nasser continued to pull strings and offer his assistance.

ANOTHER REVOLUTION

Civil war followed, pitting supporters of the YAR, known as republicans, against supporters of the imam, known as royalists. Nasser sent 40,000 Egyptian troops into Yemen to support the republicans. These soldiers were armed with modern weapons supplied by the Soviet Union. Their arsenal included airborne rockets, artillery, machine guns, tanks, and jet fighters. By contrast, al-Badr found himself at the head of a force of some 75,000 men. They were savvy guerrilla fighters who were able to strike quickly, then disappear into the mountains. Al-Badr's men carried old rifles known as *bindouks* as well as their *jambiya* daggers. Eventually, the oil-rich Saudis—who did not want Nasser to gain a foothold on the Arabian Peninsula—provided aid to al-Badr's mountain fighters.

It was a bloody fight that lasted eight years. Both sides practiced cruel and relentless tactics. Nasser's men burned villages and torched the crops of tribes loyal to al-Badr. Innocent villagers were mowed down by machine gun fire. The Egyptians also robbed the Yemenis of their meager possessions and took prisoners, jailing them in Sanaa and Cairo.

The royalists were no less vicious, showing no mercy to the Egyptian soldiers. Many hapless Egyptians captured by the Yemenis were decapitated. The Yemenis left the corpses to rot in the rocky terrain, but not before stripping the bodies of their weapons and ammunition. Egyptians who were taken captive were chained together and held in caves.

At times, the lines of loyalty were unclear. Many sheikhs would sell the services of their tribes as **mercenaries** to the Egyptians, then fight on the side of the royalists. Nasser also tried recruiting Yemenis to serve in the republican army. Soon, many of them defected. It became apparent that the civil war had turned into a battle between the Yemenis and the invading Egyptians. This was the way al-Badr tried to present the nature of the conflict to other Yemenis. "There is no civil war between royalists and republicans, only a national Yemeni war against Egyptian imperialism," he declared. "Without Egyptian troops, the republic would collapse and I could walk into Sanaa without firing a shot."

Within one year of the outbreak of the war, the International Red Cross reported that some 1.5 million Yemenis had been displaced

Abdullah al-Sallal, shown at a victory parade in 1963, was the leader of the Yemen Arab Republic, which was established after a coup in September 1962.

by the fighting. By 1965, the war had resulted more than in 100,000 deaths.

REVOLUTION IN THE SOUTH

Meanwhile, a different war broke out in the Federation of South Arabia. Great Britain dispatched soldiers to protect the federation from guerrilla fighters known as the Red Wolves, who were from the southern highlands of the Aden Protectorates and resistant to British rule. The British found themselves facing the same type of opponents in South Arabia that the Egyptians fought in Yemen:

Royalist forces man a recoilless gun on a mountain crest during the civil war in Yemen, 1964. The royalists supported Imam Muhammad al-Badr, and fought against the Egyptian troops who had entered Yemen in support of al-Sallal's Yemen Arab Republic.

quick-striking, relentless mountain fighters who showed no mercy. The war found its way onto the streets of Aden, where two high-ranking British officials were murdered. Eventually, the British were forced to suspend the constitution and impose martial law on the country.

The warfare took its toll. By 1967, unrest in South Arabia had intensified. Insurgents found a common cause with an organization called the National Liberation Front. There was no question that the NLF wanted the British out of southern Arabia, though with no ties to Nasser, they were pushed to fight the British on their own. Violence continued in the countryside as well as in the streets of the federation cities. In the summer of 1967, it became clear to the British that the NLF was winning the war. Faced with defeat and forced into deciding whether to turn southern Arabia over to Nasser or the NLF, the British chose the NLF.

On November 29, 1967, the last remaining British troops left southern Arabia. At midnight that night, the victorious leaders of the NLF proclaimed the new name of the nation to be the People's Republic of South Yemen. The leaders began implementing their plans to establish a **Marxist** regime.

EGYPT LEAVES YEMEN

In the north, Nasser became more anxious than ever to find a way out of Yemen. In June 1967, Egyptian troops suffered a devastating defeat during the Six-Day War with Israel. Responding to troop movements on its borders, Israel launched strikes against the Egyptian, Jordanian, Syrian, and Iraqi armies on June 5. The Egyptians suffered the greatest losses in the war. In less than a week, the Israelis wiped out the entire Egyptian air force—some 300 planes—and had rolled over Egyptian tank battalions. More than 15,000 Egyptian soldiers died in the fighting, and Israel held control of the strategic Sinai Peninsula.

Humiliated by the Israelis and worn down by the Yemenis, Nasser's military was bankrupt and in shambles. The Egyptian leader appealed to the Saudis and the rulers of the other wealthy Gulf states for aid. The Gulf rulers agreed to help, on the condition that Nasser pull his troops out of Yemen, which would leave the republicans to fend for themselves. The Egyptians left in October 1967. With his protectors gone, al-Sallal fled the country. He was replaced by Qadi Abd al-Rahman al-Iryani, a moderate republican, while General Hassan al-Amri became head of the republican army.

The departure of the Egyptians did not result in a quick royalist victory. With Sanaa now unprotected by Egyptian troops, al-Badr's royalists laid siege to the capital. The royalists kept up the bombardment for three months but the republicans held them off, finding much-needed assistance from Soviet forces, who finally delivered weapons they had promised. Once the siege ended, royalist troops weary of the long conflict either defected to the republicans or went home.

Meanwhile, the republicans turned on themselves. Fierce fighting broke out in the ranks among many factions. Finally, a faction headed by General al-Amri emerged victorious. By 1970, the fighting was over. Al-Badr, a Zaydi whose family held power in southern Arabia for some 1,300 years, would never rule again. Yemen's final imam was exiled to Great Britain, where he died in 1996.

And so what was left of the grand southern Arabian empire once ruled by the Queen of Sheba was now two broken, battered countries weary of civil war. In the north, a series of military coups rattled the stability of the country, while in the south a Marxist government held power.

POSTWAR YEMEN

During the 1970s, southern Arabia became a battleground in the Cold War between the United States and the Soviet Union. In the south, the Soviet Union supplied weapons to the government while the United States sought to displace the Soviets in the north.

The pact between the Soviets and the Yemeni Marxists was a curious friendship. In the former Soviet Union, the state practiced official **atheism**, which had been preached by **Communist** philosophers dating back to Karl Marx in the 1800s. In South Yemen, however, Islam was as strong a guiding force as it was in other nations of the peninsula. The people were devoutly religious and living under the *Sharia*, Islamic law that guides a Muslim's religious, political, social, and private life. In the years between 1974 and 1983, however, secular codes replaced some of the

An Egyptian tank sits disabled in the Sinai Desert, June 1967. In a preemptive strike, Israel greatly reduced the fighting capability of Egypt and its other Arab neighbors. The humbling defeat ultimately led Gamal Abdel Nasser to pull Egyptian forces out of Yemen.

Islamic codes long established by the *Sharia*, and the power of the religious establishment was severely reduced.

Elsewhere on the peninsula, business in the oil industry was booming. Following World War II, tremendous reserves of oil had been discovered in Saudi Arabia, Kuwait, Iraq, and other Gulf states. At the time, no oil had been located in either of the Yemens. Nevertheless, the oil states were in need of manpower to work in the oil fields. Thousands of Yemenis left home for work in the Gulf states. They sent their paychecks home to their families. The Yemens were still among the poorest nations on earth; nevertheless, the people of southern Arabia managed to find a modest share of the oil wealth.

Still, relations between the two Yemens remained tense. In 1972, leaders of the two countries declared their intentions to merge into one nation, but little progress was made. In 1979, war broke out between the two Yemens. The brief period of hostilities ended when the Arab League, which is the union of Arab heads of state, stepped in to mediate the dispute.

Government leaders in both Yemens failed to last very long. In the north, al-Amri ruled for a year, then was forced to resign when he murdered a photographer. Political assassinations, kidnappings, executions, and other sorts of mayhem dominated the government until 1978, when Ali Abdullah Salih attained power. Salih was able to stabilize the government and guide his nation toward democracy.

In the south, the leaders started fighting among themselves. Ali Nasir Mohammed eventually won the ensuing power struggle against Abdul Fattah Ismail, taking office as president in 1980. The People's Democratic Republic of Yemen—as it was now known—seemed to be on a path toward stability, but in 1986 a fierce civil war broke out in the country. The insurgents were led by Abdul Fattah Ismail. Following his defeat in 1980 and subsequent escape into the Soviet Union, Ismail had regrouped with his followers.

Ali Nasir Mohammed al-Hasani became president of the People's Democratic Republic of Yemen (South Yemen) in May 1980. He ruled until a 12-day civil war in 1986, when he fled the country into exile and a new government was established. Within a few years, North and South Yemen would be reunited into a single country.

Fighting broke out in January 1986 and lasted for a month. As many as 42,000 people were killed in the streets of Aden. Ismail died in the fighting and Ali Nasir was deposed, fleeing the country along with some 60,000 of his supporters.

The new president of South Yemen was Haidar Abu Bakr al-Attas. The south had never prospered under socialism and the civil war further decimated the country. What's more, in the Soviet Union the Communist system was on its last legs. Faced with incredible economic troubles of its own, the Soviet Union ceased providing aid to South Yemen. The Communist government in the Soviet Union would finally fall in 1991.

UNIFICATION

In 1988, the Yemeni socialists opened negotiations with the north to unify the country. A year later, the two sides agreed on a constitution and on May 22, 1990, the new nation was declared the Republic of Yemen. Ali Abdullah Salih became president while Ali Salim al-Baydh, a political leader from the south, became vice president. Al-Baydh's position in office meant that the southern socialists would have a role in the government.

The constitution ensured a promise of democratic government— rare in the Arab world. Some Arab countries, such as Kuwait and Jordan, permit their people to elect representatives to a legislative branch, but the executive power is held by a member of the royal family who rules for life and selects someone from his family, usually a favored son, to succeed him. But in Yemen, the constitution specifies that the president should stand for election every seven years. Other officials in the government are elected as well. However, Ali Abdullah Salih has ensured that there is no effective opposition against him.

Not everything went smoothly, though. Throughout the 1970s and 1980s, the two Yemens maintained separate armies. After unification, the army was not fully unified and old conflicts refused to die. Friction broke out between leaders of the former armies. In May 1994 the squabbles could no longer be contained and Yemen was, once again, thrust into a civil war.

The north was far more prepared for the war. From the beginning of the union, the south had been the weaker of the two states. Its former leadership was ineffective and discredited. The north had a larger population, bigger army, and many more armed tribesmen.

Aden fell to northern troops on July 7, 1994. Al-Baydh fled to Oman. More than 7,000 people died in the brief fighting while another 15,000 were wounded. Salih reached out to the southern insurgents, offering them ***amnesty*** if they laid down their arms. With no other options, many southern rebels accepted his offer.

Since the 1994 war, there have been occasional riots and violence. Some tension remains between the northern and southern regions. For example, in April 2008, riots erupted in Sanaa and near Aden, over perceived job discrimination against southerners. Over 15 protesters were injured by security forces deployed by the military. Nevertheless, Salih has presided over an era of economic growth and relative peace as he has tried to steer his country into the modern world.

The tall minaret of the al-Mudhaffar mosque towers over the city of Taizz, Yemen. The domed mosque was built during the 13th century. Islam is the official religion of Yemen, and nearly all of the people living in the country are Muslims.

Politics, Religion and the Economy

The citizens of Yemen are "guaranteed equal opportunities in the fields of political, social and cultural activities." What is more, the people of the nation live under a political system "based on social solidarity, which is based on justice, freedom and equality according to the law." These words come from the Yemen's constitution, which was adopted when North Yemen and South Yemen unified in 1990.

The 1990 constitution guaranteed that the Republic of Yemen would become one of few Arab countries governed by a popularly elected president and legislative branch. Other countries in the Arab world also have constitutions and some even invest a measure of authority in the people. But many Arab countries are ruled by members of a royal family—as is the case in Saudi Arabia, Kuwait, and Bahrain, among others—or by strongman dictators, such as Saddam Hussein in Iraq or Muammar Qaddafi in Libya. In Yemen, though, the president is elected to a term that spans seven years while members of the 301-seat House of Representatives stand for election every six years. A second legislative branch known as the Shura Council also participates in the government. The Shura Council is composed of 111 seats, and all of its members are appointed by the president.

"Democracy has become a way of life for us," said Yemen president Ali Abdullah Salih in an interview in 2000, "and the world has been witnessing Yemen's experiment with democracy from the beginning. The success of our presidential and parliamentary elections should serve as an indication of our future success in this endeavor." Still, opposition parties have yet to pose a serious challenge to Ali Abdullah Salih's presidency, and his party has maintained full control over the legislature.

Salih first rose to power in North Yemen in 1978 after President Ahmad al-Ghashmi was assassinated by a bomb hidden in a briefcase. Since then, Salih has managed to hold onto power amid the turbulent civil wars that led to Yemen's unification. During that time, he has steered his country toward democracy.

The 1999 presidential election was the first time Yemenis voted directly for their president. Under Yemen's electoral system, the constitution requires that voters be given the choice of at least two presidential candidates. However, the constitution also specifies that all presidential candidates be approved by at least 10 percent of the members of the House of Representatives. In the 1999 election, only two parties controlled enough seats to guarantee candidates would have at least 10 percent of the House's support: the General People's Congress, of which Salih is a member, and the Islah Party.

The General People's Congress is, by far, the majority party in Yemen. As a result, the Islah Party decided not to field a candidate in 1999. Still, the constitution requires two candidates for the

The flag of Yemen, with its red, white, and black horizontal stripes, is similar to the flags of several other Arab countries. Syria's flag has the same design with two green stars in the white stripe; Iraq's flag has three green stars and an Arabic inscription; and Egypt's flag has an eagle symbol in the white band.

presidential election, which meant that a member of Salih's own party, Najib Qahtan al-Shabi, had to oppose him in the election. With just token opposition from within his own party, Salih won a landslide victory with some 96 percent of the vote.

Such an overwhelming majority for one candidate led to suspicion that the election was rigged. Nevertheless, Western observers of Yemen's elections have affirmed that the balloting was staged fairly and honestly. In 2000, Robert Pelletreau, former U.S. assistant secretary of state, stated about elections in Yemen: "The United States supports democracy in Yemen. We recognize that this is a work which is continuing to develop and we support the further institutionalization of democracy in Yemen." The 2006 presidential election indicated that democracy is indeed progressing. Opposition candidates received federal funding for canvassing and television commercials, and held public rallies. Salih won the election with about 77 percent of the vote.

Due to the high illiteracy rate among Yemenis, the government has ensured that people who can't read are still able to vote by printing symbols representing particular candidates on the ballots. Every Yemeni citizen over the age of 18 is entitled to vote.

A Muslim woman wears a colorful *burka*. *Sharia*, or Islamic law, regulates how women in Yemen dress and behave in public.

The right to vote extends to Yemeni women, which is a right not granted to females in some Arab countries. Women in much of the Arab world are kept in subservient roles to men. In Yemen, though, the constitution clearly states that "citizens are all equal in rights and duties" and that "women are the sisters of men. They have rights and duties, which are guaranteed by *Sharia* and stipulated by law."

RELIGION

Sharia is Islamic law, but it is more than just a set of rules. It spells out the moral goals of a Muslim and his community. In an Islamic society, the courts look to *Sharia* for guidance when interpreting the law and enforcing justice. The *Sharia* is based on the Qur'an (or Koran) as well as other sources, including the *Sunna*, the example set by the prophet Muhammad, and the *Hadith*, a collection of writings about Muhammad. The constitution of Yemen reinforced the Qur'an and removed some of South Yemen's secular codes written in the 1970s and early '80s. The constitution states definitively that "Islamic *Sharia* is the source of all legislation."

Of course, different Islamic nations apply *Sharia* and other customs in different ways. Social custom in some Islamic countries requires women to cover most of their bodies. In Saudi Arabia and Iran, for example, women wear veils. In Afghanistan, some women wear the *burka*—a costume that completely covers their heads and

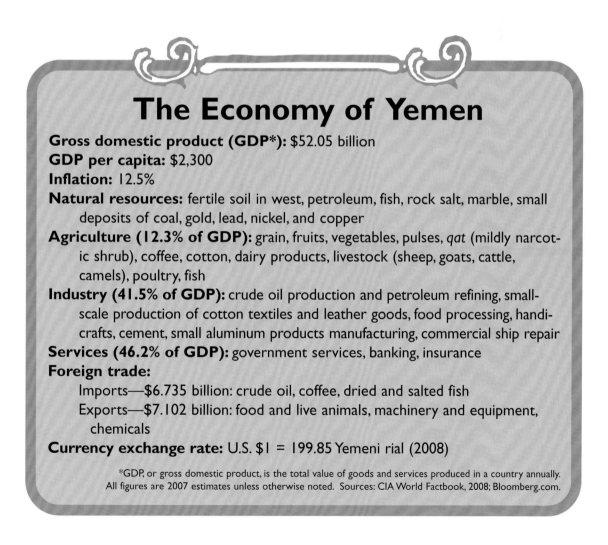

The Economy of Yemen

Gross domestic product (GDP*): $52.05 billion
GDP per capita: $2,300
Inflation: 12.5%
Natural resources: fertile soil in west, petroleum, fish, rock salt, marble, small deposits of coal, gold, lead, nickel, and copper
Agriculture (12.3% of GDP): grain, fruits, vegetables, pulses, *qat* (mildly narcotic shrub), coffee, cotton, dairy products, livestock (sheep, goats, cattle, camels), poultry, fish
Industry (41.5% of GDP): crude oil production and petroleum refining, small-scale production of cotton textiles and leather goods, food processing, handicrafts, cement, small aluminum products manufacturing, commercial ship repair
Services (46.2% of GDP): government services, banking, insurance
Foreign trade:
    Imports—$6.735 billion: crude oil, coffee, dried and salted fish
    Exports—$7.102 billion: food and live animals, machinery and equipment, chemicals
Currency exchange rate: U.S. $1 = 199.85 Yemeni rial (2008)

*GDP, or gross domestic product, is the total value of goods and services produced in a country annually. All figures are 2007 estimates unless otherwise noted. Sources: CIA World Factbook, 2008; Bloomberg.com.

most of their bodies, leaving only a thatched opening in front of their eyes. On the other hand, social customs in Kuwait are much more liberal and many women wear Western clothes in public.

In Yemen, women generally keep their faces and most of their bodies covered; it is not unusual to see women wearing *sharshafs*, long black cloaks similar to *burkas*. And yet, women in Yemen are permitted to vote, hold elective office, drive automobiles, attend college, and obtain jobs.

In many Islamic nations—including Yemen—people who violate *Sharia* risk brutal consequences. In Sudan, the sentence for armed

An illustration depicts Muhammad in a cave, receiving the word of Allah.

robbery is the amputation of the right hand and left foot. In Nigeria, the penalty for stealing is having a criminal's arm amputated. In other Islamic countries lawbreakers are still stoned or whipped.

Yemen has also imposed strict punishments for typical crimes as well as infractions of *Sharia*. In 2001, Amnesty International, the human rights watchdog group, reported that Yemen police routinely use torture to extract confessions to crimes. Some crimes—such as adultery and slander—can be punished through flogging. People who face the death penalty in Yemen have had their sentences carried out in public squares.

Yemen has 23 million citizens, virtually all of them Muslims. There are also Hindus, Christians, and Jews in the country, but together they number no more than a few thousand. There are fewer than 300 Jews living in Yemen today, a small remnant of what was a large and thriving community before 1948. Most Jews in the Middle East emigrated to Israel following the creation of the country in 1948.

In Yemen, though, Jews were traditionally treated with hospitality by the Zaydi imams, who were greatly influenced by the prophet Muhammad's belief that Jewish thought contributed to Islamic doctrines. During the 1970s, Yemeni leaders asked Jews who had left the country to return, hoping to make use of their skills in the technical trades.

The religion established by Muhammad in the early seventh century is known as Islam, which can be loosely translated to mean "submission to Allah." To accept Islam is to accept five basic laws known as the five pillars. The first pillar is the *Shahada*, which calls on Muslims to faithfully recite a declaration of faith: "There is no god but Allah, and Muhammad is His Prophet." The second pillar is *Salat*, the duty to pray five times a day. The third pillar is *Sawm*, a required fast between sunup and sundown during the holy month of Ramadan. The fourth is the principle of donating to charity, known to Muslims as *Zakat*. The final pillar is the *hajj*, the pilgrimage to Mecca, which is the birthplace of Islam. Those Muslims that are capable are obligated to make the hajj at least once in their lifetime.

The words of Allah, as recorded by Muhammad, came to be known as the Qur'an. This became the doctrine that governs the Islamic faith. It took several years for Muhammad to recite the laws; when he spoke, his words were copied down on scraps of leather, flat stone tablets, and even camel bones by his followers.

Yemen's Muslims are almost split evenly between Shiites and Sunnis, the two sects of Islam that have been rivals for some 1,300 years. The Sunnis make up the majority of the world's Muslims— more than 80 percent. Shiites comprise a much smaller share of the world Muslim population; most of their members live in Iran but many also live in countries like Iraq, Lebanon, Bahrain, and Yemen.

Following the death of the prophet Muhammad in 632, the Qur'an gave no clear method of succession for leadership of the faith. Two factions emerged in a contest for leadership. The Sunnis were led by the Omayyads, an aristocratic family from the Arabian city of Mecca. In Arabic, the word *Sunni* is derived from the term for "tradition." The Sunnis favored selection of the successor by Islamic leaders, who would elect the *khalifa*, or caliph. The Shiites—a name drawn from the Arabic word for "partisan"—were led by Ali, Muhammad's son-in-law, who believed the caliph should be a member of the Prophet's family. Ali would eventually become the fourth caliph; when he was murdered the Shiites insisted the next caliph should be one of Ali's sons. The Sunnis prevailed, though, and the succession passed out of Ali's family.

Over the years the Shiites have lived under a stricter interpretation of Islamic law and have preferred their rulers to be members of the clergy. The Zaydi imams, who ruled Yemen for more than a thousand years, were a subsect of Shiites. As a result, Yemen retains a large Shiite population.

ECONOMY

Yemen is one of the poorest countries on Earth, a fact that can be attributed to the strife and civil war that lasted for decades; the failures of the south's Marxist government during the 1970s and 1980s; and the country's inhospitable climate and terrain, which has made agriculture in Yemen a difficult venture.

Most of the nations on the Arabian Peninsula sit atop tremendous oil reserves that have made their people wealthy. The Kuwaitis

Hundreds of displaced refugees wait in long lines for food and water from relief workers, shortly after Iraq's invasion of Kuwait. The government of Saudi Arabia, angered by Yemen's support of Saddam Hussein's aggression, expelled hundreds of thousands of Yemeni workers from the country.

and Qataris, for example, enjoy some of the highest standards of living in the world. Oil has only recently been discovered in Yemen, though, and because of the long-lasting civil war as well as the country's lack of technology and resources, extracting it from the ground has not been easy. What's more, low prices for petroleum in the late 1990s further slowed the growth of Yemen's emerging oil industry.

In the early years of the 21st century, prices escalated, and Yemen is finally beginning to realize its potential as an oil producer. The Canadian Occidental Oil Company and the Texas-based Hunt Oil Company have made major investments in Yemen's oil industry. In addition, the American oil giant Exxon Mobil Corporation is a member of an international consortium of energy companies developing a $6-billion project to obtain natural gas from Yemen. Still, Yemen is a small player among the world's oil producers. In 2005, Yemen pumped some 400,000 barrels of oil per day. By contrast, the Saudis produce about 10.5 million barrels per day.

No question, the wealth from oil production will take time to find its way to the Yemeni people. The national unemployment rate is about 35 percent. A major reason for Yemen's high unemployment can be attributed to the country's response to Iraq's invasion of Kuwait in 1990. Yemen sided with Iraq and supported Saddam Hussein in the subsequent Persian Gulf War. At the time, some 850,000 Yemenis were working in Saudi Arabia, most of them in the oil industry. The Saudis sided with Kuwait because they feared the Iraqis would move their campaign of aggression into Saudi Arabia. In the end, Yemen paid the price for supporting Iraq. Saudis angrily expelled the Yemeni workers from their country, and Western countries cut off aid to Yemen.

It is estimated that of the 56 percent of the people who hold jobs in Yemen, about 2.8 million work on farms that produce *qat*, coffee, cotton, tobacco, grains, livestock, and poultry. The remaining 2.2

million of employed Yemenis work on fishing vessels, in the oil fields, or in the country's factories, many of which produce textiles and leather goods. Yemen has a small mining industry that produces coal, gold, lead, nickel, and copper. Just 3 percent of the country's land is capable of being farmed. About 68 percent of the tillable land—some 2.7 million acres—is in farm production. Farms produced 3.6 million tons of crops in 1999.

Most of Yemen's imports are obtained from other nations on the Arabian Peninsula, particularly the United Arab Emirates and Saudi Arabia, although Yemen also obtains goods from the United States, Australia, China, and Japan. Yemen exports most of its goods to consumers in China and Thailand. Other export customers include Australia, Saudi Arabia, Japan, and the United States.

The currency in Yemen is the Yemeni rial. In 1995, 40 rials equaled one U.S. dollar. In mid-2008, 199.85 rials equaled one U.S. dollar, meaning that the rial has lost spending value when measured against American currency. The weak value of the rial is yet another contributing factor to Yemen's economic woes.

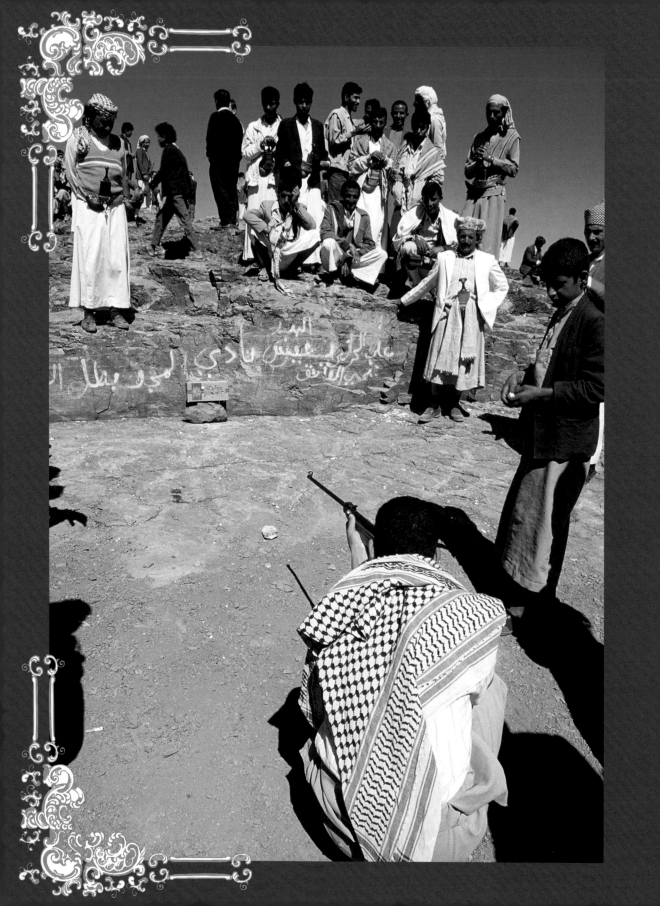

A group of men participate in a shooting contest during a wedding celebration in a Yemeni village in Wadi Dahr. Guns are common in the country; nearly everyone has a weapon and knows how to use it.

The People

It is said that Yemen is a land of 23 million people and 50 million guns.

Guns are easy to come by in the country. They are readily available at most *souqs* (outdoor markets) and the government doesn't control who owns them. In the United States, the constitution guarantees the right to bear arms; nevertheless, federal, state, and local laws regulate the use and ownership of guns and strict penalties are imposed on citizens who violate the nation's gun laws. In Yemen, the country's constitution guarantees no right of the people to own guns and yet most Yemenis have personal gun collections that would impress even the most avid gun collector in America. Yemen's civil wars provided opportunities for the tribes to arm themselves, and efforts by the government to restrict guns have had little success.

One *souq* merchant, Abdullah al-Awsa, told a journalist,

"The Prophet, God's blessings on him, said, 'Teach your children to swim, to shoot, and to ride.'" Muhammad had bows and arrows in mind when he offered that wisdom; nevertheless, today it is not uncommon in Yemen to find automatic weapons, grenade launchers, and even anti-aircraft missiles for sale at a *souq* and to hear the rat-a-tat-tat of gunfire as customers test the weapons while they haggle over prices with *souq* merchants.

Visitors to Yemen may see a citizen carrying a Russian-made Kalashnikov machine gun slung over his shoulder, as well as the traditional *jambiya* dagger stuffed into the sash around his *futa*, an ankle-length kilt worn by most Yemeni men.

Many Yemenis reached adulthood while their country was locked in civil war. As such, they learned how to use guns to defend themselves while in combat. Although there has been not been a war in recent years, Yemenis still insist on keeping their guns close. They have found other uses for guns: some people may, for example, fire them off as a form of celebration. It is not uncommon to see a Yemeni honor a bride and groom with a salute of gunfire during a wedding reception, or charge into the street with guns blazing skyward to announce the birth of a child.

Despite their history of warfare as well as their fondness for firearms, Yemenis are generally not a violent people. They much prefer talking over disagreements and reaching a compromise than in challenging one another with weapons drawn. Some Yemenis claim that disputes may be resolved when the parties involved sit down together and share *qat*.

QAT

The popularity of *qat* ("pronounced cot") is undeniable: it is estimated that some 80 percent of the adult population of Yemen chews *qat* leaves. *Qat* is a common shrub that emerged in the latter half of the 20th century as Yemen's primary cash crop. Every

Most of the people of Yemen live along the coast, with the highest concentration near the capital city, Sanaa. For the most part, the northern and eastern areas of the country are sparsely inhabited.

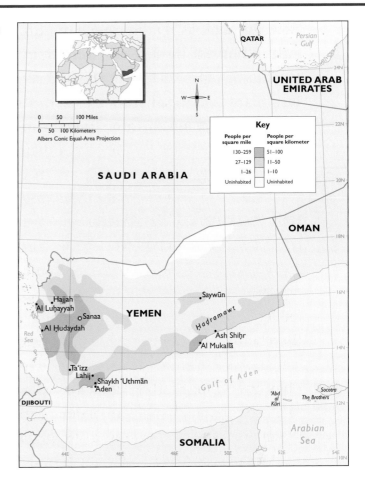

afternoon, a majority of Yemeni men disappear into their homes where, surrounded by friends or business associates, they while away the hours stuffing *qat* leaves into their cheeks. It is a custom that dates back some 500 years or more.

Qat has a stimulating effect. Many Yemenis believe it clears their minds and puts them in a blissful mood that helps ease their troubles, settle their differences, or just make pleasant talk with their friends. *Qat* is illegal in the United States and most other countries. In America, it is regarded as a controlled substance subject to the same laws as **marijuana** or **cocaine**.

Qat must be chewed within 48 hours of its harvest for the user to obtain the stimulating effect. Since *qat* is grown virtually nowhere except Yemen and a handful of African nations, it is difficult to harvest the leaves, ship them to America, and get them into the hands of users before the potency wears off. Also, *qat* is a seedless plant—a circumstance that has made it impossible to smuggle a crate of *qat* seeds into America to establish an illegal *qat* farm.

Therefore, outside Yemen *qat* is chewed in just a few neighboring countries on the Arabian Peninsula and Africa, where authorities take a dim view of the practice.

That isn't the case in Yemen, however. Many homes feature a *mafraj*, which is a common room where *qat*-chewing often takes place. The room is usually lined with cushions, where men can recline and enjoy one another's company. Some Yemenis enjoy chewing *qat* on the roof of their home.

Westerners who have tried *qat* report that the leaves taste similar to almonds. Because *qat* makes the chewer thirsty, water or soft drinks are usually served during a chewing session, while coffee or tea may be served afterwards. By no means is *qat* reserved for use strictly in the home. Although alcoholic beverages—prohibited by Islamic law—are not present in

The People of Yemen

Population: 23,013,376
Ethnic groups: predominantly Arab; but also Afro-Arab, South Asians, European
Religions: Muslim including Shaf'i (Sunni) and Zaydi (Shia), small numbers of Jewish, Christian, and Hindu
Language: Arabic
Age structure:
 0–14 years: 46.2%
 15–64 years: 51.2%
 65 years and over: 2.6%
Population growth rate: 3.46%
Birth rate: 42.42 births/1,000 population
Death rate: 7.83 deaths/1,000 population
Infant mortality rate: 56.27 deaths/1,000 live births
Life expectancy at birth:
 total population: 62.9 years
 males: 60.96 years
 females: 64.94 years
Total fertility rate: 6.41 children born/woman
Literacy (age 15 and older): 50.2% (2003 est.)

All figures are 2008 estimates unless otherwise noted.
Source: CIA World Factbook, 2008

A Yemeni man chews *qat*, a stimulant that is legal—and very popular—in Yemen.

public or in the home, visitors to Yemen will often see men as well as many women going about their business at the *souqs* or strolling home from work with large pinches of *qat* in their cheeks.

Since the *qat* leaves lose their kick so soon after they are picked from the stalk, Yemenis obtain their daily supplies just before they expect they will chew. Most *qat* is obtained from street vendors or *souq* merchants who themselves procured their supplies that morning from *qat* farmers. There is always a lot of haggling over the price of *qat*. Leaves harvested from the bottom of the plant are cheaper than leaves pulled from the top of the *qat* plant, which can grow as tall as 20 feet (6 meters). The reason? Yemenis believe the leaves at the top of the plant are more tender and potent.

Most Yemenis are hard-pressed to pay the price for the top leaves, though. A bundle of the top leaves could cost the equivalent of $40 or $50, which is far too expensive for the average Yemeni making a living on a fishing boat or in a leather factory. And so, most Yemenis must make do with the bottom leaves.

Before unification in 1990, the Marxist-dominated government in South Yemen strictly regulated *qat*, permitting it to be grown in limited amounts. After unification, though, the regulations were dropped and *qat* farming spread throughout the south. (It had never been regulated in the north.) Now, it is estimated that some 270,000 acres in Yemen are devoted to *qat* farming, and that *qat* production accounts for 25 percent of Yemen's gross domestic product as well as 16 percent of the country's employment.

FOOD AND DRINK

Yemenis also enjoy coffee and, in fact, believe they grow the tastiest coffee in the world. The port city of Mocha was so important to the coffee trade in the 18th and 19th centuries that the city's name eventually became an English language synonym for coffee as well as the term for its dark brown color.

Coffee was first grown in Yemen about A.D. 1000. Arab traders discovered coffee beans in Africa and learned that they could brew a tasty drink by boiling the beans. They gave the beverage the name *gahwah*, which is translated to "that which prevents sleep" (clearly, the early Arab traders recognized the potency of the coffee ingredient **caffeine**). In 1690, Dutch traders started shipping coffee out of Mocha, establishing the south Arabian city as the center of the Middle East's coffee trade.

Most coffee consumed in the United States is grown in South America, so many Americans would not recognize the flavor of coffee that is enjoyed by Yemenis. In South America, plump and juicy coffee beans are grown on plantations situated amid vast rainforests. In Yemen, where there is a small amount of rainfall, the coffee beans produced are small and extremely hard. Yemeni farmers believe the dry conditions of their country give the compact little beans a tart and tangy taste. The coffee produced from the beans is thick and creamy with a bittersweet, chocolate-like flavor.

Yemenis also enjoy tea, and it is a beverage typically consumed during meals. People of different cities have different preferences when it comes to tea. For example, in Aden, people prefer an especially sweet tea. They will pour sugar into the water before boiling it and adding the tea leaves. They may also add spices such as cardamom, which is similar to ginger. Cakes or biscuits are often enjoyed with the sweet tea.

In recent years *qat* has been finding its way to the streets of American cities. Although the leaves of the plant dry out and lose their effects within 48 hours of harvest, *qat* dealers in Yemen have found that by wrapping the *qat* in banana leaves and sprinkling it with water during the journey, the *qat* can retain some freshness. A bundle of *qat* leaves has a street value of $40 in New York City, and is nicknamed "Arabian tea."

People in Hadhramaut prepare tea by first boiling water over a fire or electric range in a large open pan. Once the water boils, a smaller kettle containing water and strong tea is dangled above the large pan, which heats the tea in the smaller kettle. The tea is then poured into tiny glasses. Hot water from the large vat is also added to the small cups.

Some popular foods of Yemen are *saltah*, a hot stew made of meat and herbs usually served at lunch; *hori*, a spicy stewed beef; *hawayil*, which is a variety of spices such as peppercorn, caraway, saffron, and cardamom that are blended together and used as a seasoning; and *bint al-sahn*, a honey cake enjoyed after a meal.

Naz: Yemeni Sports Hero

He was born in Great Britain and maintains citizenship there. Yet Naseem Salom Ali Hamed, the featherweight boxing champion of the world for five years, is regarded as a national hero in Yemen.

Naseem is known to his fans as Prince Naseem or simply "Naz." His father is a Yemeni citizen who emigrated to Britain before Naseem was born. His talent as an athlete was recognized when he was a young boy, learning to box when he was just seven years old.

He soon became a rising talent among young boxers. He had his first professional fight in 1992. Through May 2003, he fought 37 times, compiling a record of 36 wins and one loss. Thirty-one of his wins have been by **knockout**, many of them coming in the early rounds. In 1996 he floored boxer Said Lawal in a bout held in Scotland after just 35 seconds in the first round. A year later, in a bout in Manchester, England, Naseem decked his opponent Billy Hardy after just 93 seconds in the first round. As a featherweight, Naseem fights in one of boxing's lightest weight classes. For a typical fight, he'll usually weigh in at less than 126 pounds.

Yemeni fans remain ever loyal to Naseem, even though he maintains British citizenship and makes his home in New York City. In 1999 his image was featured on a Yemen postage stamp. He has also received a national award of honor from President Ali Abdullah Salih.

Through Naseem, Yemenis can boast of success in the world of boxing, but they have been far less successful in other sports. Soccer is the national sport of Yemen. Children play the sport in the streets of the cities as well as the dusty squares of their mountain villages. Internationally, though, the Yemenis have not fared well. No team from Yemen has ever advanced past the preliminary rounds in World Cup competition. From time to time, Yemen has sent athletes to the Olympic Games in various competitions, but no Yemeni has yet won a medal.

The boxer Prince Naseem, or Naz, is a sports hero to many people in Yemen.

Bread is baked in large circular loaves. Yemenis tear hunks off the loaf and dip them into *fuul*, which is similar to chili sauce.

POPULATION GROWTH

Yemen is experiencing a population explosion. In 2001, the population of the country grew by 3.4 percent to just over 18 million. If that trend continues, the population of Yemen, which stood at roughly 23 million in 2008, could double within 20 years.

There are many factors contributing to the population growth. The country's recent political stability is certainly one such f actor. With an end to the many civil wars, the families of Yemen finally have an opportunity to grow. Also, the modernization of the country has certainly led to the fast growth rate: with Yemenis receiving more advanced medical care, the citizens are able to endure illnesses and diseases that in the past were often fatal.

Still, modern medicine is largely out of reach to most Yemenis. There is just one doctor for every 4,530 Yemeni people. That lack of medical expertise has led many Yemenis to seek cures from healers who use ancient rituals to treat illnesses. One such cure employed by the ritual healers involves drawing blood from an ill person by making an incision in the skin, then placing a ceramic conical horn over the cut that will then be heated to create suction. Once the healer determines he has created a vacuum inside the horn, he opens a tiny hole in the tip of the cone and, using his mouth, sucks out the infected blood.

EDUCATION

School attendance in Yemen is low—only 57 percent of children between the ages of 6 and 15 attend school. That number includes 79 percent of the young male population and 33 percent of the young female population.

For decades, the curriculums of Yemen's schools were limited to teaching the Qur'an, but starting in the 1970s, North Yemen and South Yemen each established public schools with broader programs. Since so many Yemeni workers did not have the right training, teachers had to be imported from other countries.

The Yemenis were able to rely on the neighboring oil states to help pay the teachers' salaries for nearly two decades. But when the Yemen government backed Iraq in the Persian Gulf War, the Saudis, Kuwaitis, and other Gulf states dropped their support for Yemeni schools. The salaries of some 30,000 teachers were cut off, forcing them to leave their jobs and return to their home countries. Faced with a significant teacher shortage, the Yemeni government has struggled to fill jobs and find the money to pay salaries. This crisis is a primary reason why more than half of the population is illiterate, including 70 percent of all women.

THE THEATER AND THE ARTS

As one of the world's oldest civilizations, many historians believe that Yemen may have been the birthplace of the dramatic arts. Archaeological excavations near the Marib dam, which was constructed 2,500 years ago, have unearthed remnants of what historians believe was a theater. Historians have also uncovered works of poetry and other literary works that date back to 2000 B.C., making them older than any works produced by the ancient Greeks and Romans.

In modern times, Yemenis have been far less successful in the arts. In 1999, the much-beloved Yemeni poet Abdullah al-Baradouni died at the age of 70. Al-Baradouni was the author of 12 books of verse, often using his poetic craft to criticize the government. Blind since the age of six after contracting **smallpox**, al-Baradouni was a strong advocate for democracy and women's rights, and had been imprisoned for his beliefs many

There are many Yemenis living in the United States; one large community is located in Lackawanna, New York, which is located near Buffalo. In September 2002, after investigation by the FBI and CIA, five men of Yemeni descent were arrested in Lackawanna; they were accused of being part of an al-Qaeda sleeper cell.

times during his life. Over the years, he received death threats from Muslim fundamentalists.

In addition to publishing verse, he also wrote books on politics, literature, and folklore. Two weeks before his death, he remarked the government of Yemen had not done enough to support the arts. "It does not possess a cultural project to enlighten the society," he said.

Yemen's most successful contemporary performing artist is the singer Ahmad Fathi. He began developing as a musician by first playing the lute, a stringed instrument in the class of the guitar and violin. Eventually, Fathi switched to singing and has recorded many traditional Yemeni songs.

Traffic in Sanaa, the largest city in Yemen. Sanaa is the capital, and is also an important business center.

Communities

The most striking feature of any city in Yemen is its architecture. The country is famous for its tower houses, buildings with up to nine stories that boast a truly original vertical plan. Tower houses can be seen in Sanaa, Aden, and elsewhere. Many cities and even remote villages have imposing edifices that were erected at a time when southern Arabia was the most modern civilization on the planet. At a time when the people of North America were living in caves or covering their teepees with buffalo skins, the people of Al Hajjara in the Haraz Mountains near Sanaa were living in multi-storied complexes made of granite, basalt, and brick. **Mosques** in Yemen feature tall **minarets** with domed roofs. In the mountains, many majestic palaces sit atop tall peaks, with access to them made available over stoned bridges that arch from peak to peak.

SANAA

"There are three earthly paradises," the prophet Muhammad is recorded as saying. "Merv of Khurasan [province of northeast Iran], Damascus of Syria, and Sanaa of Yemen. And Sanaa is the paradise of these paradises."

Of course, Muhammad spoke of a completely different Sanaa than what Yemenis know in the 21st century. Today, Sanaa is an overcrowded, dirty city whose residents enjoy few modern conveniences. The lightning-fast growth of Yemen's population has brought about sudden change throughout the country, but particularly in Yemen's capital. In "Old Sanaa," which is in the center of the city, visitors can find narrow streets weaving alongside homes, mosques, and other buildings dating back some 2,000 years or more. There are, for example, some 14,000 "tower houses" in Old Sanaa. These homes are five or six stories high. The bottom floor has the storage supplies, the middle floors are where the family resides, and the top floor is reserved for the *mafraj*, where *qat* is usually chewed.

Outside the old section, newer homes are crowded together with businesses. Overcrowding remains one of Sanaa's biggest problems, as the city's population has doubled every four years since 1970. In 2004 the population was recorded at nearly 1.8 million residents.

The quick growth of Sanaa has produced some positive results. For example, the city boasts a $50-million Sheraton hotel, built with government assistance, as well as many modern homes and commercial buildings. Since Sanaa is the capital, the president's residence, parliament, courts, and most of the government's other major buildings are located in the city. Foreign countries maintain their embassies in Sanaa as well.

Many problems have also accompanied Sanaa's quick growth, however, including poor sanitation. The city's water system is dirty and inadequate. Most residents, fearing the presence of disease-carrying parasites, boil their water before drinking it. Raw sewage often spills on city streets.

OTHER CITIES

No city in Yemen comes close to the size of Sanaa. The second-largest metropolis, the port city of Aden, has only about one-third the population of Sanaa. An estimated 588,938 people lived in the city in 2004. Like Sanaa, Aden is plagued by a growing population struggling to find available space in a city that dates back to biblical times. Aden has always based its livelihood on its seaport. Merchant ships and fishing boats make their way in and out of the harbor each day. In order to bring business into Aden and boost its revenue, the government convenes in the city for three months each year.

Another large city in Yemen is Taizz, which had about 466,968 people in 2004. The city's architecture exhibits foreign influences because the people of Taizz and the surrounding region have worked outside Yemen for generations. Taizz also served as the residence of Imam Ahmad during his rule. Although there are many old-style *souqs* in Taizz, there are also many modern shopping centers. The people of Taizz regard themselves as much more multinational than the residents of Sanaa and Aden. Many of Yemen's businesses have established their headquarters in Taizz.

Al Hudayda, with an estimated 409,994 residents in 2004, ranks

Some Yemenis believe the city of Aden may be as old as human history itself—at least as it is revealed in the Old Testament. They point out the similarity of the name of Aden with Eden, the birthplace of humanity described in the Book of Genesis. They also believe the graves of Cain and Abel are somewhere in the city.

as Yemen's fourth-largest city. Al Hudayda is a port city on the coast of the Red Sea. As with Aden, this city's economy is based on the traffic of merchant ships and fishing boats. After Yemeni citizens were expelled from Saudi Arabia in 1990, many of them settled in Al Hudayda, which is just down the coast from Jidda and other large Saudi cities.

Yemen is divided into governorates, similar to how America is divided into states. There are 19 governorates in Yemen. The largest is the governorate of Taizz, with more than 2.5 million people. The smallest is the governorate of Al Mahra, which is located in the far eastern end of the country along the Oman border. Al Mahra is composed mostly of desert and it recorded only 96,800 inhabitants in 2006. The city of Al Ghayda, with just 13,000 people, is the largest community in the governorate. Most people in Al Mahra live along the coast of the Arabian Sea and make their livings aboard fishing vessels.

MARIB

A very small city in Yemen is Marib, which is located in the governorate of the same name. In the Queen of Sheba's day, Marib was the capital of the Saba empire. Once the great dam collapsed and the empire of the Sabaeans crumbled, Marib became no more than a sleepy community of 4,000 in the Yemen highlands. In 1986, though, the Hunt Oil Corporation of Texas discovered oil near Marib, and once again the city became an important part of life in Yemen. Getting the oil out of Marib has proven to be a difficult undertaking, however. A pipeline laid to the city has been sabotaged many times by Arab tribes prompted by various disputes with the government.

There is important archaeological research conducted in Marib. In recent years, artifacts, pottery, artwork, and other remnants of the Sabaean culture have been unearthed. One important discov-

Five pillars mark the site of the ruins of an ancient temple, known as Mahram Bilqis, near Marib. Although tradition links the temple with the Queen of Sheba, the structure was not built until the 8th or 7th century B.C., several hundred years after her meeting with Solomon.

ery was the ruins of the Mahram Bilqis, which in English translates to "Temple of Sheba." The ruins are believed to be some 3,000 years old. American archaeologists first unearthed the temple in 1951, but political unrest abruptly halted their work. Not until the 1970s

were archaeologists permitted to return. In 2000, Canadian archae-
ologist Dr. William Glanzman updated reporters on the progress of
the dig he was leading. There was still a lot of work ahead for his
team, as according to his estimates, researchers have unearthed
less than 1 percent of the Temple of Sheba: "We have an enormous
job ahead of us. . . . We're trying to determine how the temple was
associated with the Queen of Sheba, how the sanctuary was used
throughout history, and how it came to play such an important role
in Arab folklore."

Once the site is completely excavated, the government of Yemen
hopes to restore and reconstruct sections of the Temple of Sheba so
visitors can see the temple as it appeared during the height of the
Saba dynasty. That will be a considerable undertaking for the
people of Yemen. Said Glanzman, "In many respects, the Queen of
Sheba's kingdom was the cradle of the Arab civilization and the
Mahram Bilqis was at the very heart of this kingdom. This temple
may well be considered the eighth wonder of the world."

CELEBRATIONS

Yemenis are devout Muslims and, as such, they observe the holy
month of Ramadan, the ninth month in the Islamic year. Because
the Muslim calendar is based on the moon and not the sun, the
Islamic year is 11 days shorter than the Christian year, which
means the month of Ramadan changes through the seasons.

According to Muslim tradition, Ramadan was the month in
which the Qur'an was revealed to Muhammad. During Ramadan,
Muslims abstain from food and drink during the daylight hours and
are encouraged to devote more time to meditation, studying the
Qur'an, and strengthening their relationships with friends and
family members. At night, people often stay up late socializing.

To properly observe Ramadan, most Muslims rise before dawn
and eat a pre-fast meal known as the *suhoor.* After sunset, they

break the fast with a meal known as the *iftar*. The 27th and last night of Ramadan is known as *Laylat al-Qadr*, or "Night of Power." The night is sacred because it marks the revelation of the first holy verse of the Qur'an to Muhammad.

Ramadan is also a time of gift-giving. During the final three days of the month, Muslims in Yemen and many other countries celebrate by exchanging gifts and visiting one another's homes. This period is known as Eid al-Fitr. Children receive *eidah*, money or candy given by older relatives. Many children also dress in costume and knock on doors in their neighborhood seeking candy, much as American

In the Khawlan area, about 21 miles (35 km) from Sanaa, armed Yemeni tribesmen hold hands during a traditional dance. They are participating in ceremonies during the second day of Eid al-Fitr, which marks the end of Ramadan.

children observe Halloween. They also may light firecrackers, while women and young girls sit together and listen to music.

Other religious holidays include days that mark the birth of the prophet Muhammad and the day of his ascension, which change each year according to the Islamic calendar. Another religious celebration is the four-day Eid al-Adha, which is the feast of sacrifice and completion of the pilgrimage to Mecca, the birthplace of Islam.

Secular holidays celebrated in Yemen include January 1, New Year's Day, and May 1, Yemen's Labor Day. Yemenis celebrate several holidays that mark turning points in their country's political history. Before the two Yemens were united, each country had its own holidays. As such, holidays celebrated by people in the south had little significance to people in the north. Nevertheless, after the 1990 unification, in an attempt to forge closer ties, government leaders of the north and south decided that the regions should observe each other's official holidays. Those holidays include Revolution Day, which is observed on September 26. The day marks the uprising against Imam Muhammad al-Badr in 1962, which is significant to northerners but has little relevance in the south, since at the time the south was the Federation of South Arabia and was under the rule of the British. A holiday that southerners cherish is Independence Day, celebrated on November 30. This date marks the eviction of the British from the south in 1967.

May 22 is National Unity Day—the national observance of the 1990 reunification of the two Yemens. National Unity Day is commemorated with parades, the largest of which occurred during the 2000 celebration, which marked the 10th anniversary of reunification. For the celebration, some 100,000 Yemenis participated in a parade through the streets of Sanaa.

Some communities have their own celebrations. In Al Faydami, a small town in the governorate of Al Mahra, people celebrate the coming of autumn each year, which marks the end of the rainy monsoon season. Folk artists gather in Al Faydami to give music and dance performances. The town holds banquets as well as many sporting events, including soccer games, foot races, and volleyball matches. The most popular events in Al Faydami during the autumn festival are the camel races, which draw spectators from throughout the governorate.

The people of Aden celebrate a festival honoring a 15th-century holy man named Abu Bakr ibn Abdullah al-Aydarus. It is said that al-Aydarus once saved the life of a ship and its crew with his super-human powers. From the shore he flung a stick—with which he normally used to clean his teeth—to plug a crack in the sinking ship miles out at sea. Legend also says that the great holy man saved the people of Aden from famine by making the sky rain milk.

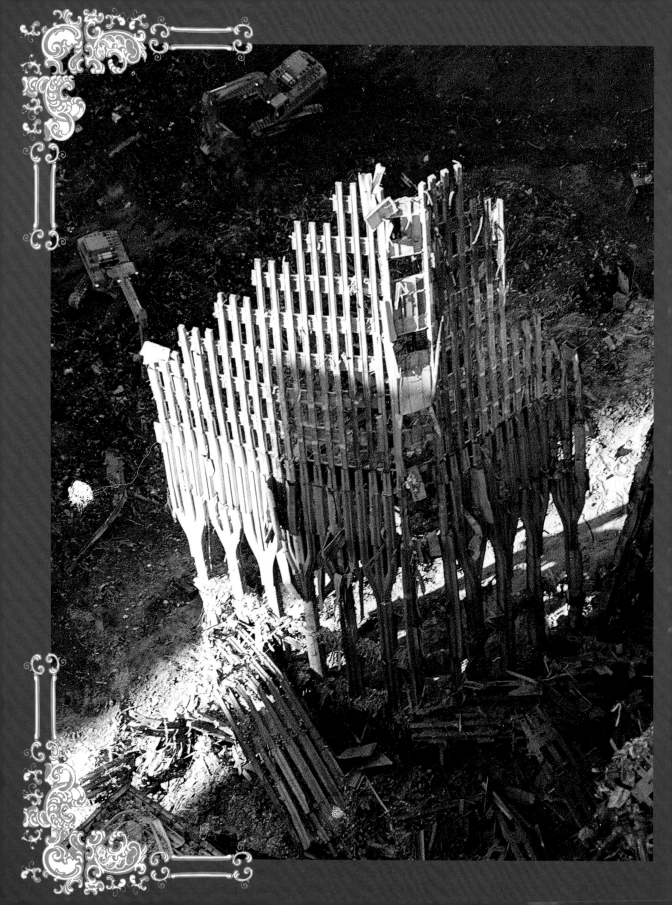

An aerial view of the last remnants of the World Trade Center after the September 2001 terrorist attacks. The attacks were planned and executed by the al-Qaeda network, which has long supported terrorists operating in Yemen. The U.S. State Department has issued several warnings to Americans visiting the country.

Foreign Relations

*F*ollowing the terrorist attack on the *Cole*, the U.S. State Department advised Americans to leave Yemen. The State Department also issued an official travel warning, which added Yemen to a list of countries in which Americans are not regarded as safe. The State Department reinforced these warnings following the al-Qaeda network's attack on the World Trade Center in New York and the Pentagon in Washington.

In another State Department travel warning issued on March 18, 2002, all U.S. citizens in Yemen were advised to "pay close attention to their personal security and to take those actions they deem appropriate to ensure their well-being." Specific places that should be avoided were those associated with foreigners like "the Sanaa trade center, American-affiliated franchises, restaurants and shops . . . in Sanaa and, in Aden and elsewhere, at restaurants and hotels frequented by **expatriates**." Another report in November 2002 reiterated the earlier warning and stated that the "security threat to all American citizens in Yemen remains high." The State Department's warnings were based primarily on intelligence gathered about terrorists with ties to the al-Qaeda network.

Although a lack of security in Yemen failed to help prevent the *Cole* disaster, the government of President Salih has attempted to make up for its neglect. It provided assistance to the more than 300 FBI agents and other American law enforcement officials dispatched to Yemen to investigate the *Cole* bombing. Also, in June 2001 police in Yemen arrested eight men who were charged with planning to blow up the American embassy in Sanaa.

The attack on the *Cole* was a terrible shock for many Americans, especially those not attuned to recent developments in the Middle East. However, authorities in America and other Western nations suspected Yemen was dangerous turf for visitors several months before the bombing of the *Cole* in Aden harbor.

KIDNAPPING IN YEMEN

The first display of hostility in Yemen toward Westerners occurred in December 1998, when a group of Muslim extremists kidnapped 16 British tourists. With its hostile climate and rugged terrain, Yemen would hardly seem a likely destination for tourists. But when the civil war ended and the two Yemens unified, the ancient country, with its ruins and artifacts dating back to the Queen of Sheba's time, became something of a popular destination for hardy and adventurous travelers. By the late 1990s, some 70,000 tourists a year were visiting Yemen.

A day after the abductions, Yemeni police tracked the kidnappers to their hideout. A gunfight ensued. Two of the kidnappers were killed and three arrested. Later, six more kidnappers were apprehended in a mountain hideout. As for the tourists, four of them died in the police assault.

The suspects were convicted. Most were sentenced to lengthy prison terms, but the alleged ringleader, Zein al-Abidin al-Mihdar, was sentenced to death. Al-Mihdar, head of a radical Islamic group called the Aden-Abyan Islamic Army, admitted to kidnapping the tourists. In October 1999, the Yemeni government carried out al-Mihdar's sentence by setting him before a firing squad in Sanaa.

For the next several months, the Aden-Abyan Islamic Army threatened to avenge al-Mihdar's execution by carrying out terrorist strikes against British as well as American citizens. The extremists also said the U.S. and Great Britain were to blame for the suffering of the Iraqi people. The two countries had led the international coalition that drove the Iraqis out of Kuwait in 1991. They also had been instrumental in keeping up the trade blockade against Iraq that successfully weakened Saddam Hussein's regime. Finally, American and British warplanes had policed the no-fly zones around Iraq that were designed to bottle up Saddam's air force. If another war were to break out between a Western coalition and Iraq, U.S. security organizations would need to closely monitor the activities of the Aden-Abyan Islamic Army.

On October 13, 2000, a day after the terrorist attack on the *Cole*, a bomb exploded outside the British embassy in Sanaa. No one was injured in the bombing, but the incident alarmed British officials, who believed their long alliance with America was the root cause behind the decision to attack the embassy.

The December 1998 kidnappings of the British tourists was not the first instance of abduction in Yemen. In fact, during the past decade some 150 foreigners have been kidnapped in the country. However, prior to the incident involving the British citizens, none of the abductions were carried out for political purposes. Instead, tribal sheikhs in Yemen would order their members to snatch hostages off city streets or rural roads either because they believe most foreign visitors are wealthy and their relations back home can afford huge ransoms to pay for their freedom, or they want the government to address specific grievances of a tribe or small community.

Not until the British citizens were killed had any violence been committed against foreign hostages. In fact, captors usually treat their hostages snatched for ransom with a surprising level of hospitality. After spiriting them away to their mountain village, the kidnappers usually untie their hostages and allow them the freedom to walk without escort within the confines of the village.

Shaker al-Ashwal, a Yemeni living in America who manages a website guide on Yemen, has written about kidnapping in his native

In November 2002, a CIA-operated Predator drone fired a missile that destroyed a truck said to be carrying six al-Qaeda leaders, among them Qaed Senyan al-Harthi (center, wearing checkered headcloth, shown standing next to Osama bin Laden in this video frame from CNN). The attack was carried out with the knowledge of Yemen's government.

country. For the 40 tourists that experts predicted would be kidnapped in 1998, he offered the following advice:

> [E]njoy your time as a hostage, your hosts (kidnappers) will treat you not as a kidnapped person, but as a guest. If you're lucky you'll get kidnapped by a rich tribe and you'll be fed lambs and exotic fruits and return home carrying a nicely ornamented Yemeni dagger and maybe some jewelry for that significant other.

Typically, negotiations between diplomats from the visitor's home country and tribal leaders take about a week. The two sides haggle until they finally agree on a ransom price. Then, the hostage is released so that he or she can return home and impress friends with stories of the "ordeal." Following his release, Italian tourist Giorgio Bonanomi said, "Too bad it's not possible to organize holidays like this, because it was fantastic."

In recent years, authorities in Yemen have tried to put an end to the kidnappings by adopting strict laws that include the death penalty for violators. Still, the kidnappings continue.

YEMEN AND THE UNITED STATES

Yemen has been involved in few armed conflicts with other countries, largely because its militaries have remained totally engaged with the country's frequent and long-lasting civil wars. Whenever Yemen has found itself taking sides in an international conflict, the country's leaders have often picked the losing side. In the 1970s, the leaders of the Marxist-dominated government in South Yemen provided support for a rebellion against the royal family of Oman that proved unsuccessful.

In 1991, Yemen made the even larger mistake of backing Iraq in the Persian Gulf War. Although Yemen sent no troops to aid Iraq, Salih refused to join the American-led coalition that liberated Kuwait from the Iraqi invaders, a decision that would have devastating consequences. Foreign aid to Yemen provided by the

United States as well as the Saudis, Kuwaitis, and the other Gulf states was immediately cut off, costing the Yemen government treasury some $3 billion. As many as 850,000 Yemenis working in the Gulf states, most of whom were oil field laborers, were kicked out and forced to return home, where few jobs awaited them. Yemen's support for Saddam Hussein angered American political leaders. Relations between the U.S. and Yemen remained icy until 1994, when the United States backed President Salih's government in the civil war waged that year. Over the next six years, relations

This North Korean ship was intercepted by Spanish and U.S. military forces in December 2002; when it was searched, it was found to be carrying Scud missiles to Yemen. The U.S. permitted the ship to proceed to Yemen after the government promised not to sell the missiles to any third party.

continued to improve. In April 2000, a friendly meeting took place between President Salih and President Bill Clinton at the White House.

Following the World Trade Center and Pentagon bombings, American diplomats appealed to President Salih to become an ally in the war on terrorism. In November 2001, Salih was again invited to Washington, where he met with President George W. Bush. Then in March 2002, Vice President Richard Cheney visited Sanaa for a brief meeting with Salih. The American vice president did not expect a warm welcome from the Yemenis. Just days before Cheney arrived in Sanaa, the *Yemen Observer*, an English language newspaper, reported that only 35 percent of Yemenis welcome U.S. military presence; the *Yemen Times* reported similar results. Some Yemeni political leaders vocalized the people's frustration. Sheikh Abdullah bin Hussein al-Ahmar, speaker of the Yemen parliament, bluntly stated that Yemenis have surrendered to the United States because "it is the strongest in the world."

Cheney spent just two hours in Yemen, not even making it past the airport in Sanaa. Nevertheless, his brief meeting with Salih produced an agreement from Yemen's head of state that the country would support America in its war against al-Qaeda and would not permit followers of Osama bin Laden to seek refuge in Yemen's rugged mountains. In return, the Americans agreed to send military advisers to Yemen, where they would help train members of the Yemen military and police in anti-terrorist warfare. "We have increasingly developed in more recent months very close bilateral relations between the United States and Yemen," Cheney announced after meeting with the Yemeni president. Salih was equally satisfied with the meeting. "The fight against terrorism is paramount and should continue," he said.

The Arab nations had little, if any, incentive to back the losing side in this war. By the time Cheney arrived in Yemen, American

The U.S. secretary of defense, Donald H. Rumsfeld (left) escorts Yemen's president, Ali Abdallah Salih, into the Pentagon. Since the terrorist attacks on September 11, 2001, Yemen's government has worked with the United States to find terrorists and break up their operations.

troops had pounded Afghanistan for months, ousting the ruling Taliban regime from power. The Taliban had been al-Qaeda's close ally, sheltering the extremist group and enabling Osama bin Laden to establish training camps for terrorists.

ARAB NATIONS

Yemen has signed a number of international treaties, some of which include bans on the use of land mines. The devices are buried just below the ground and explode when enemy soldiers steps on them. Sadly, many civilians are killed or suffer the loss of limbs from land mines because long after fighting has ended, the mines remain buried and hidden. Because of its long history of civil wars, Yemenis have often fallen victim to land mine explosions. A Yemeni government study done in 2000 determined that 592 villages fall within areas where land mines still exist, and that there could be as many as 100,000 land mines buried in Yemen. Much of American's foreign aid to Yemen, which amounts to about $2 million a year, is spent on efforts to uncover and remove land mines.

Although Yemen has long maintained a tolerant attitude toward its own Jewish citizens, the country's leadership has steadfastly supported the Palestinians in their ongoing conflict with Israel. President Salih has often issued statements harshly condemning Israel and has directed his government to organize demonstrations in support of the Palestinians. Just a few days before the *Cole* bombing, some 50,000 Yemenis participated in a public demonstration to protest Israel's refusal to relinquish control of the territory known as the West Bank, which the Palestinians demand as their homeland.

Yemen's closest neighbor is Saudi Arabia, a country with which it shares a 906-mile (1,458-km) border, most of which cuts through remote desert. Much of the border has remained in dispute since the Treaty of Taif in 1934, which awarded Yemen the Tihama coastal plain while allowing the Saudis to keep the Asir and Najran regions of the western highlands. The terms of the Taif treaty expired in 1974, though it was renewed at five-year intervals for the next 20 years. In 1994, the two sides failed to renew the treaty and resumed the earlier border dispute.

Salih was anxious to avoid total war with the Saudis. In 1995, the two sides began negotiating terms, and they finally completed a border treaty in July 1996. Under the agreement, the Saudis got to stay in Najran and Asir, while the Yemens were granted territory in the country's eastern portion, which was mostly desert. In June

A U.S. expert instructs Yemeni soldiers in minesweeping techniques near Aden. According to some estimates, there are between 60,000 and 100,000 land mines in Yemen, and much of the U.S. financial assistance to the country is spent clearing these dangerous minefields.

2000, the two sides signed the final truce in the Saudi city of Jidda.

During this period, Yemen faced another volatile territorial dispute with a neighboring country. In 1995, Eritrea claimed the Hanish Islands in the Red Sea. The tiny African nation located just across the Red Sea and north of the Bab el Mandeb sent troops to the islands and raised its flag. Instead of repelling the invaders, the Yemenis requested the United Nations to mediate the dispute. The

UN ruled that the islands should remain part of Yemen's territory, but that Eritrea should be granted fishing rights around the islands. Eritrea was satisfied with the ruling, since these rights were basically what it sought anyway.

As Yemen moves into the 21st century, it continually hopes to one day share peace with its Middle Eastern neighbors. Arab-Israeli relations remain cold, and Iraq is facing pressure from the international community. But now that Yemen has stronger diplomatic ties to the West, and a more stable approach to the democratic process, it has a closer chance of avoiding the strife and isolation of its brutal past.

CHRONOLOGY

1000 B.C.: The Kingdom of Saba in southern Arabia emerges with a powerful and influential culture.

950–930 B.C.: The Queen of Sheba and King Solomon of the Israelites form a friendship that ensures Saba's domination of the resin trade.

500 B.C.: Sabaeans erect the dam at Marib, which remains standing for 1,000 years.

A.D. 300: The Himyarites gain dominance over southern Arabia, replacing the Sabaeans as the ruling culture.

570: The prophet Muhammad is born in Mecca on the Arabian Peninsula.

628: Badhan, Persian governor of southern Arabia, converts to Islam.

9th century: A Shiite Muslim offshoot group known as the Zaydis takes power in southern Arabia, establishing a state that would rule off and on until 1962.

13th century: Marco Polo visits the island of Socotra off the coast of Yemen.

1538: Ottoman Turks establish control over Arabia, including Yemen.

1618: The British begin exporting coffee from Mocha.

1637: The Ottomans are kicked out of southern Arabia by the Zaydi ruler Muayyad, who establishes a unified Yemen that exists until 1731; it is the last time the country would be united until 1990.

1728–31: The al-Abdali prince revolts and murders the reigning imam's governor; the al-Abdali family establishes its own independent state in Lahij, north of Aden, which divides Yemen once again.

1833: Ottoman Turks return to rule Yemen under Ibrahim Pasha.

1839: The British navy under Commander Stafford Bettesworth Haines seizes Aden and establishes British rule over South Yemen that will last until 1967; the region under the British becomes known as the Aden Protectorates.

1919: After losing on several fronts in World War I, the Turks relinquish their rule over North Yemen.

1934: Zaydi imam Yahya signs a treaty acknowledging British control over South Yemen; after waging a short war with the Saudis, Yahya grudgingly agrees to sign the Treaty of Taif, which establishes a common border between North Yemen and Saudi Arabia.

CHRONOLOGY

1948: Yahya is assassinated by the Free Yemenis, a rebel group committed to ending his despotic rule; Yahya's son Ahmad suppresses the ensuing revolution and executes its leaders, then declares himself the new imam.

1951: Archaeologists discover the ruins of the Temple of Sheba buried near Marib.

1953: The British propose democratic self-rule for the Aden Protectorates.

1955: Ahmad puts down a coup and executes his brother Abdullah, one of the conspirators.

1956: Yemen, Egypt, and Saudi Arabia sign the Jidda Defense Pact.

1959: British designate the Aden Protectorates the "Federation of South Arabia" and establish a timetable to turn the government over to local authority.

1962: Ahmad dies and a military coup topples the government of his son, Imam Muhammad al-Badr; civil war breaks out in the north between royalists loyal to al-Badr and republicans loyal to Egyptian president Gamal Abdel Nasser; Egyptian troops assist the republicans in the war.

1967: British troops leave southern Arabia; a Marxist-dominated regime assumes power and designates the country the "People's Republic of South Yemen" (later changed to the "People's Democratic Republic of Yemen"); Egyptian troops leave North Yemen where the civil war continues.

1970: Civil war ends in the north with a republican victory; al-Badr is exiled to Great Britain.

1978: Military leader Ali Abdullah Salih is named president of North Yemen following the assassination of President Ahmad al-Ghashmi.

1986: Civil war erupts in the south, ending in the eventual demise of the Marxist regime.

1988: The two Yemens open negotiations on reunification.

1990: Unification talks end with the establishment of the Republic of Yemen; Salih is named president; former southern leaders are given positions in the new government.

1993: Elections are held for a new legislature; southerners are removed from their positions in the government.

CHRONOLOGY

1994: Civil war again erupts in the south as insurgents try to break up the Republic, but the rebellion is quickly quashed.

1998: Sixteen British tourists are kidnapped in Yemen by Muslim extremists; four hostages die in the subsequent shootout between the police and kidnappers.

2000: On October 12, 17 Americans are killed when a terrorist bomb explodes alongside the USS *Cole*, which had been anchored in the port of Aden; the al-Qaeda terrorist network is soon identified as the terrorist group behind the blast; Yemen and Saudi Arabia finally sign a treaty defining their borders.

2001: Police in Yemen arrest eight men for planning to blow up the U.S. embassy in Sanaa; on September 11, more than 2,000 people are killed in the al-Qaeda attacks on the World Trade Center in New York City and the Pentagon in Washington.

2002: U.S. vice president Dick Cheney meets with Salih in Yemen; Salih commits to cooperating with the U.S. in the war on terrorism, in return for which America sends military advisers to Yemen.

2003: In January, Yemen parliament members urge the Yemeni people to protest against the U.S.-led campaign to attack Iraq.

2006: In September, President Ali Abdullah Salih is reelected with more than 77 percent of the vote. International observers say that the presidential election was conducted fairly.

2007: Yemen discusses becoming a member of the Gulf Cooperation Council, a organization of Arab states in the Persian Gulf.

2008: On September 1, a suicide car bombing kills 16 people at the U.S. embassy in Sanaa. Islamic Jihad, a group reportedly linked to al-Qaeda, claims responsibility.

GLOSSARY

amnesty—the act by which a government pardons an individual or group, usually for political offenses.

atheism—disbelief in the existence of God.

autocratic—ruling a people or nation with unlimited authority.

caffeine—a chemical present in coffee that stimulates the heart and central nervous system.

cocaine—an illegal narcotic obtained from cocoa leaves.

Communist—having the characteristics of an economic or political system based on collective ownership of property.

contingent—a representative group of things or people.

coup—short for coup d'etat, a sudden illegal overthrow of one government for another, usually by means of force.

equator—the imaginary circle around the Earth, equally distant from the North and South Poles, that separates the Northern and Southern Hemispheres.

expatriates—citizens of a nation who choose to leave their homeland and establish their homes in a foreign country.

fallow—an agricultural term applied to a farm field that is left untilled or unseeded.

fundamentalist—a person whose religious beliefs are based on literal interpretations of the Bible, the Qur'an, or other doctrine.

guerrilla—a fighting strategy in which soldiers act secretly and strike quickly, usually from hideouts deep in the jungle or the mountains.

Gulf state—a state bordering the Persian Gulf.

harem—quarters kept in Muslim households in which wives, concubines, or female servants are expected to live.

knockout—in boxing, a victory scored by a fighter whose opponent is beaten so badly he is judged incapable of finishing the contest.

marijuana—dried leaves from the hemp plant that can produce a narcotic euphoria when smoked.

Marxist—having the qualities of a classless society and economic system advocated by Karl Marx, a Russian 19th-century philosopher.

GLOSSARY

mercenaries—professional soldiers engaged in military conflict who take up arms but have no allegiance to the side they fight for other than the pay they receive.

minarets—high towers found atop mosques that feature a balcony from which an individual summons worshipers to prayer.

mosques—places of worship in the Islamic faith.

quarantine—a place where people are detained and monitored in order to prevent the spread of disease.

sheikhdoms—territories under the control of an Arab chief.

smallpox—a virus that includes high fever, vomiting, and sores that often leaves scars or pockmarks in the victim's skin after recovery.

tropic of Cancer—the line of latitude that is approximately 23.5 degrees north of the equator.

tropic of Capricorn—the line of latitude that is approximately 23.5 degrees south of the equator.

FURTHER READING

Caton, Steven C. *Yemen Chronicle: An Anthropology of War and Mediation.* New York: Hill and Wang, 2005.

DiPiazza, Francesca Davis. *Yemen in Pictures.* Minneapolis: Lerner Publishing Group, 2008.

Dresch, Paul. *A History of Modern Yemen.* Cambridge, England: Cambridge University Press, 2000.

Field, Michael. *Inside the Arab World.* Cambridge, Mass.: Harvard University Press, 1994.

Hansen, Eric. *Motoring with Mohammed: Journeys to Yemen and the Red Sea.* Boston: Houghton Mifflin Company, 1991.

Lunt, James. *The Barren Rocks of Aden.* New York: Harcourt, Brace & World, 1967.

Mackintosh-Smith, Tim. *Yemen: Travels in Dictionary Land.* New York: Picador, 1997.

McLaughlin, Daniel. *Yemen.* Guilford, Conn.: Bradt Travel Guides, 2007.

Miller, Judith. *God Has Ninety-Nine Names: Reporting from a Militant Middle East.* New York: Touchstone, 1996.

Nyrop, Richard, ed. *The Yemens: Country Studies.* Washington, D.C.: American University, 1986.

Schmidt, Paul, trans. *Arthur Rimbaud: The Complete Works.* New York: HarperPerennial, 2000.

http://www.yementimes.com

Site of the weekly English language newspaper published in Yemen. It includes news and features about Yemen as well as editorials, interviews with newsmakers in Yemen, and letters to the editor from Yemeni citizens as well as readers who live in other countries.

http://www.state.gov/r/pa/ei/bgn/35836.htm

Visitors to the U.S. State Department's background notes on Yemen can learn about the country's geography, government, people, economy, history, and current political situation.

http://www.yemenembassy.org

Yemen's embassy in Washington features abundant information on the economy, government, and cultural life of the country. Visitors can play a 46-second audio recording of Yemen's national anthem and cast their ballots in a poll gathering support to name Old Sanaa one of the "New Seven Wonders of the World."

http://www.cole.navy.mil

The USS *Cole* maintains this Internet site. Visitors can learn about the navy ship and its history as well as the memorial in Norfolk, Virginia, dedicated to the 17 American crew members who lost their lives in the October 2000 terrorist attack on the ship.

INDEX

Numbers in **bold italic** refer to captions.

INDEX

The **FOREIGN POLICY RESEARCH INSTITUTE (FPRI)** served as editorial consultants for the MAJOR MUSLIM NATIONS series. FPRI is one of the nation's oldest "think tanks." The Institute's Middle East Program focuses on Gulf security, monitors the Arab-Israeli peace process, and sponsors an annual conference for teachers on the Middle East, plus periodic briefings on key developments in the region.

Among the FPRI's trustees is a former Secretary of State and a former Secretary of the Navy (and among the FPRI's former trustees and interns, two current Undersecretaries of Defense), not to mention two university presidents emeritus, a foundation president, and several active or retired corporate CEOs.

The scholars of FPRI include a former aide to three U.S. Secretaries of State, a Pulitzer Prize–winning historian, a former president of Swarthmore College and a Bancroft Prize–winning historian, and two former staff members of the National Security Council. And the FPRI counts among its extended network of scholars—especially its Inter-University Study Groups—representatives of diverse disciplines, including political science, history, economics, law, management, religion, sociology, and psychology.

DR. HARVEY SICHERMAN is president and director of the Foreign Policy Research Institute in Philadelphia, Pennsylvania. He has extensive experience in writing, research, and analysis of U.S. foreign and national security policy, both in government and out. He served as Special Assistant to Secretary of State Alexander M. Haig Jr. and as a member of the Policy Planning Staff of Secretary of State James A. Baker III. Dr. Sicherman was also a consultant to Secretary of the Navy John F. Lehman Jr. (1982–1987) and Secretary of State George Shultz (1988).

A graduate of the University of Scranton (B.S., History, 1966), Dr. Sicherman earned his Ph.D. at the University of Pennsylvania (Political Science, 1971), where he received a Salvatori Fellowship. He is author or editor of numerous books and articles, including *America the Vulnerable: Our Military Problems and How to Fix Them* (FPRI, 2002) and *Palestinian Autonomy, Self-Government and Peace* (Westview Press, 1993). He edits *Peacefacts*, an FPRI bulletin that monitors the Arab-Israeli peace process.

HAL MARCOVITZ is a journalist for *The Morning Call*, a newspaper based in Allentown, Pennsylvania. He has also written about Kuwait for the MAJOR MUSLIM NATIONS series. He lives in Chalfont, Pennsylvania, with his wife, Gail, and daughters Ashley and Michelle.